Peruvian-Chinese Cuisine

FAMILY SECRETS

Experience the flavors of Peru!

KATIE CHOY

A portion of the proceeds from the sale of this book
benefit the Peruvian American Medical Society

Lydia Inglett Ltd. Publishing
Award-winning publishers of elegant books

Family Secrets

Peruvian-Chinese Cuisine

Experience the flavors of Peru!

ISBN: 978-1-938417-21-4

© 2015 Copyright Katie Choy

To order additional books, view new recipes and join our community: www.katiechoy.com

Photography: Francesca Choy, Rogelio Choy, M.D.
Digital Designer: Armand Choy
Editor: Trudi Miklos
Assistant Editor: Stefan Choy

Published by Lydia Inglett Ltd. Publishing
www.lydiainglett.com
www.starbooks.biz
301 Central Ave. #181
Hilton Head Island, SC 29926
info@starbooks.biz

To order more copies of this or any of our books, visit our on-line bookstore

www.STARBOOKS.biz

The place for beautiful, thoughtful gift books

Lydia Inglett Ltd. Publishing

Award-winning publishers of elegant books

This book is dedicated to my mother-in-law,
Consuelo, and my mother, Joanne, who instilled
in my husband and me the importance of family
mealtime. *Family Secrets* is not only a cookbook, but
a celebration of enjoying food with the ones you love.

Katie Choy

Table of Contents

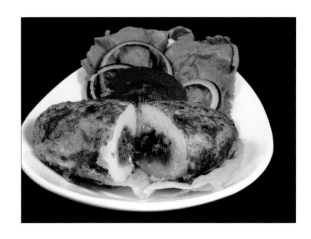

Welcome to the Empire of the Incas

Some Secrets Are Better Left Unknown, Others Are Not …

I INVITE YOU INTO THE MYSTERIOUS empire of the Incas to explore their well-seasoned secrets that remained unique to the land for thousands of years. The world today is a more flavorable place since the discovery of Peruvian food. Let me show you how you, too, can share these treasures with your family, and watch them flourish!

Consuelo Aragón de Choy was born in the mountains of Arequipa, Peru, and learned to cook from her Inca

Consuelo Aragón de Choy and the author, Katie Choy

mother. Her husband, Francisco "Pancho" Choy was Cantonese and loved to prepare his native Chinese foods. Together, they had the flavors of both worlds, and their foods began to blend. Blending is very common in Peruvian culture because Peru has a very large Chinese population. Did you know that Peru is world-renowned for its cuisine? If you have never been there, put it at the top of your list of places to visit. Oh, and while you are there, be sure to enjoy a Pisco Sour!

I, on the other hand, have an Irish mother, a German father, and I spent my childhood in a small rural town north of Pittsburgh, Pennsylvania. I grew up enjoying freshly picked garden vegetables and traditional meat-and-potato dinners. While everything had the flavor

A young Francisco
"Pancho" Choy, c. 1940

that comes only from freshly-grown and harvested produce, it didn't have the sauces and zeal that I have come to love today! As a gringa newlywed with a Peruvian husband, my taste buds took on a whole new experience when I first tasted the extraordinary flavors of Peruvian cuisine; it was love at first bite! I would watch my mother-in-law Consuelo cook and write down some of her recipes, but once I started having children, that went by the wayside. I was "just too busy," as we all say. I kept thinking, I will learn, but not today. As they say in Peru, "Mañana!"

A few years later, on one of her visits, Consuelo fell and broke her leg, requiring emergency surgery. She faced a difficult recovery, and initially, she was not able to cook. Losing her independence and no longer being able to provide her family's meals caused her to become depressed. Eventually, she realized that she could sit in the kitchen with her leg elevated, cutting and slicing, while teaching me how to prepare her native foods. Her face came alive with pleasure at the fact she was still needed! During this time, I realized her "secrets" could have been lost forever! This unexpected revelation inspired me to write this book. I already have a wonderful collection of recipes from my parents, including special ones passed through several generations, but I also wanted to have a memoir of Consuelo's and Pancho's creations. And so, I began compiling as many recipes as she could recall.

This collection may differ slightly from Consuelo's original recipes. They have been altered and adapted to what we have

"Pancho" and Conseulo,
c. 1960

Consuelo Choy still having fun cooking at 90 years young!

available, the same as the original Inca foods were altered and adapted by the Spaniards, Chinese, and many other immigrants. Additionally, we have a son with a severe peanut allergy and some of these recipes traditionally incorporated peanuts. Out of necessity, we eliminated them, or used other nuts. All throughout the world, this is how cooking has evolved; it is an ongoing adaptation process.

On one of our visits to Peru, Consuelo, at 88 years young, cooked for us each evening so I could complete my recipe list. I asked her if she does this on a daily basis. Sadly she replied, "Not so much." It is not because she doesn't want to, or isn't able to, but because her

Best cooking lesson ever, making papa rellena with Abuelita! Francesca and Consuelo Choy c. 2001

family simply orders a pizza or throws together a sandwich. As each generation passes, the art is slowly dying. What a tragedy.

I am not a trained chef. I am not a professional writer. I am not even Peruvian! But I do love to cook and have spent nearly 20 years learning, preparing, and perfecting these authentic recipes. Most of us have heard the old joke about "turning into your mother," generally as something of an insult. But one of the best compliments I received from my husband was the day he came home from work, and I was busy in the kitchen preparing a Peruvian dinner. He stopped, looked at me, and said, "I think you are turning into my mother," with a big warm smile on his face! What better way to keep your husband happy than by serving his favorite childhood meals?

I think many of us, including myself, fall into the trap of believing we need the latest and greatest in kitchenware. When I think of Consuelo, I imagine her mixing by hand and cooking her distinctive foods over a kerosene Primus stove, as my husband vividly remembers. In reality, we don't need modern conveniences to have a family meal; we simply need *the family sitting down together*, to have a family meal! The real *"Family Secret"* is to put your love into every dish whether you slaved all day, or whether it came from a box. I invite you back into the kitchen to explore a whole new world of flavor. Enjoy and celebrate mealtime everyday ...

Katie

Essentials

History

Spices and Foods

Equipment

Habits

Adobe walls of Huaca Pucllana, Lima, Peru, built by a pre-Incan culture, developed between 200 AD and 700 AD.

History

THE PERUVIANS LOVE TO EAT, and eat a lot, especially potatoes! They are very proud of their food and love to share it with the world. I find it rather ironic, because the Peruvian food we know today has been a result of the world sharing with Peru!

I can probably guess what you are thinking: what is Peruvian food and why is it so special? My answer, "How much time do you have?" I could literally go on for page after page explaining the history and the foods, but you can research that another time. I will sum it up for you briefly, so you will have more time to get started cooking and even more importantly, eating!

The Butterfly Effect is what comes to mind with the history of Peruvian food. We are able to date it back to

Huaca Pucllana ruins are located in the Miraflores district of Central Lima, Peru. This was an important ceremonial and administrative center of the Lima Culture indigenous civilization.

4000 BC to the Pre-Inca's diet consisting mainly of corn, potatoes, and chilies, along with spices, squash, and beans. These staples are still used today and make certain dishes notably Peruvian. As time moved forward, the Incas conquered many regions, and their Empire became enormous. Each region had very different foods and flavors. The coastal region obviously was rich in seafood, the Amazon was abundant in fresh water fish and exotic fruits and plants, and the Andean region was full of indigenous people using mostly foods related to the Pre-Incas, including

**Ready for a parade at the
Plaza de Armas, Lima, Peru.**

the meat of guinea pigs and alpacas. Fast-forward to the 1500s and the invasion by Francisco Pizarro. The colonization by the Spanish introduced European diets, consisting of mainly livestock, wheat, and rice. The Spanish also brought over African slaves who did much of the cooking, and the blending of flavors progressed. The butterfly wings continued flapping into the 1800s with the influx of Chinese and soon after, the Japanese. I think you are catching on, yes, those Asian foods fused with the already melting pot of flavors.

Now you see why it can be difficult to briefly answer, "What is Peruvian food?" It is the exquisite blend of flavors from four continents. My simple summary: "Harmonizing the unique flavors of the Peruvian chile, with meat or fish, served over a bed of rice, and topped with lots of potatoes!"

Quechua woman and
llama, Cuzco, Peru.

Spices and Foods

**Look for these at Latin and Asian markets, or order online.
See website for direct links.**

ACEITUNAS DE BOTIJA are known as Peruvian olives, despite the fact they are not native to Peru. They were introduced by the Spanish over 500 years ago and differ from the more commonly known Spanish olive. They are larger, meaty, and dark purple in color, similar looking to a Kalamata olive, yet different in taste.

Ajis (pronounced \ä-'hē\) are native to South America and are more commonly called peppers, a misnomer started by Christopher Columbus. The two are not even related. The more correct name is called "chiles." Peru has several varieties and they range in flavor and heat. I will explain the varieties used in my recipes. They can be purchased in different forms, from fresh, dried, powdered, to paste. My recipes are all based on jars of paste.

Peruvian aji chiles

• **Aji Panca** is dark red/brown. It has minimal heat, and a delicious smoky flavor.

• **Aji Amarillo** is yellow and has a fair amount of heat. It is believed to be the most commonly used chile in Peru. It adds flavor, color, and heat to your dishes.

TIPS FOR SUCCESS

• Consuelo taught me a trick years ago to keep my jars of paste fresh and free of any molds. Before placing an open jar of paste into the refrigerator, pour a small amount of oil on top. This produces an airtight barrier and extends the life of your paste, unless you are like us and go through it so quickly it doesn't have a chance to spoil.

Huacatay paste, Aji Panca paste, and Aji Amarillo paste

• **Aji Rocoto** chiles are round, red, and have large black seeds. They have a reputation of being very hot. Because fresh ones can be difficult to find where I live, Consuelo took a traditional Peruvian recipe using rocotos and adapted it to American bell peppers. When we travel to Peru, I love to get the real thing, and yes, they live up to their reputation!

"Pimiento Rellenos a la Consuelo" a.k.a. Stuffed Bell Peppers, Consuelo Style. See Tips for Success, page 67.

TIPS FOR SUCCESS

• If you are fortunate enough to have access to dried aji, you can easily make your own paste. For the aji panca, take a package of dried chiles and soak in warm water for at least 20 minutes. Split open and remove and compost seeds. Place chiles in blender with 3-4 cloves of garlic and ½ teaspoon of cumin. Start with a small amount of water and blend until smooth with a ketchup-like consistency. Do the same for the dried aji Amarillo, but omit the garlic and cumin. These pastes freeze well.

• Rocoto chiles make a wonderful spicy dipping sauce. Take 1 jarred rocoto, remove seeds, drain well, and press between paper towels to squeeze out excess liquid. Place in food processor with 2 cups mayonnaise, sour cream or yogurt, ½ teaspoon cumin, 1-2 teaspoons lime juice, ½ teaspoon salt, process until smooth and keep refrigerated.

Choclo is an Andean variety of corn common to Peruvian meals. It is not as sweet as American corn and the kernels are very large. I describe it as "meaty corn." It is an accompaniment to several dishes in the book. It usually comes frozen, either on the cob, or loose kernels. However, if you are unable to find it, you may substitute American corn on the cob.

Ginger is used very often in these recipes and is a staple in my refrigerator. It adds that special zing that makes the dish unmistakably Asian. I always use fresh ginger root as opposed to ground ginger.

Heinz ketchup is not from Peru, but I'm from Pittsburgh, so it is a must for these recipes to be successful!

Huacatay is an herb native to Peru. Sometimes it is referred to as black mint and it falls within the marigold family. It adds flavor and depth to sauces. Even though it is called black mint, I do not feel it has any taste similar to mint, so I would not suggest using mint as a substitute for huacatay.

Limes are used so often in these recipes and add the perfect amount of acidity and flavor to make your mouth water. Limes are not native to Peru and were believed to have been brought over at the time of the Spanish invasion. They quickly became incorporated into the native dishes to give them the wonderful flavors we know today. I have the luxury of having my own Key lime tree in the yard; however, most people have to purchase them from the grocery store. Unfortunately, most stores sell small green, un-ripe Key limes. A truly ripe one is golf ball size or larger and bright yellow like a lemon. They produce

Deliciously juicy and ripe Key limes.

a large amount of juice. If you have purchased the small green ones and wondered why they weren't very juicy, now you know why. My Key limes are like gold to me!

Maiz morado is a beautiful dark purple variety of corn and is used to produce a wonderful beverage.

Potato starch and corn starch both work well as thickening agents. The main difference is that cornstarch holds up better in heat. This becomes useful when preparing foods that thicken over a long cooking process. Cornstarch becomes a little more opaque and can leave behind a noticeable taste. As for potato starch, it

Produce from a local street vendor, Miraflores, Peru.

breaks down quicker when exposed to heat for a long period of time. Thus, it is best used to thicken a sauce in the last minutes of cooking. It is also lighter and provides a nice silkiness and gloss to the sauce. All of Consuelo's recipes are thickened at the end, therefore, potato starch is a better choice. However, either one will produce a successful sauce.

Quinoa has been a staple in the Andean diet since pre-Columbian times! It looks like a grain, acts like a grain, but it is not a true grain; it is a "pseudo cereal." Quinoa is very high in complete protein, low in fat, and is referred to as a superfood. For some reason, Consuelo did not prepare it for us, but I make it for my family in a variety of ways, from a sweet, hot breakfast food, to salads, or as a replacement for ground beef. Find your own favorite way of enjoying quinoa with a plethora of recipes on the internet!

Rice is a must on a Peruvian or Asian dining table. It originated in China and has provided important nutrition as it spread throughout the world. Many of these recipes are served with rice. I typically use long grain white rice with a 2:1 ratio in the preparation. Choose your favorite rice to make with these meals, but always be aware of your water to rice ratio and adjust as needed.

TIPS FOR SUCCESS
• My father-in-law had a fool-proof way to check the right amount of water when making rice. He would put the rice and water in the pot, and then measure by putting his index finger in the liquid until it touched the rice. If the water was at the level of his first joint, it was the perfect amount of water every time.

Equipment

LONG COOKING CHOPSTICKS are a wonderful tool when frying and make food easy to turn in the hot oil. Make sure they are real bamboo as opposed to plastic so they can withstand the heat.

Using a Potato Ricer makes me feel like kid again! Remember squeezing Play-Doh through the holes of the press? That's the feeling you get when you "rice" a potato. I highly suggest purchasing this kitchen essential if you plan on making some of these recipes. If you are in a pinch, or unable to get one, you can always use the large holes of a box grater, or use a hand potato masher, but the ricer is so much more fun!

Potato Ricer

Spider Strainers are a handy tool in cooking because you can easily remove and quickly drain large amounts of food from hot oil or boiling water. They are an oval shaped wire skimmer attached to a long wooden handle. The name comes from the spider web pattern.

Steamers produce foods that are healthy, delicious, and remain moist. Steamers all work on the same principal: boiling water contained in a closed compartment to bathe the food in steam without directly touching the water. There are several ways to achieve this from high end to simple.

• **Built-in steam ovens** can be a good investment if you do a lot of cooking. Restaurants usually have steam ovens and they are also a wonderful way to re-heat foods without becoming dry.

• **Rice steamers** are a rather inexpensive counter-top appliance that steams more than just rice. You may want to take into consideration the size if you plan on doing steamed foods for a large family.

• **Bamboo steamers** are a traditional Chinese way of steaming. They can be stacked one atop another for multiple foods to be steamed at the same time.

• **Create your own steamer** using a few simple kitchen items. The key is to keep the food above the water. You can put this together quickly by taking a wok, a slow-cooker, or a large Dutch oven, put something heatproof on the bottom that will lift the plate, such as metal cookie cutters, a steamer basket, or simply some crumpled balls of aluminum foil. Fill the water just to the level of the chosen item, place your plate on top holding the food, and cover with a lid. Bring to a boil and time according to recipe. Yes, it's that simple!

Woks have been around for over 2000 years; they come in a variety of sizes, styles, and materials. Manufacturers will insist their design is "New and improved," but I believe the ancient Chinese did it right the first time, as described below.

Before you get started, you may be wondering, "Do I have to use a wok for these recipes?" Not necessarily, but using not only a wok, but also the right kind of wok, can make a big difference in the outcome of your stir-fry. Stir-frying is done over very high heat, using minimal oil. If you do not have access to a wok, make sure you use a heavy-duty pan that can take the high temperature. Keep in mind that woks can be used for many other forms of cooking besides stir-fry. They are great for deep-frying, steaming, poaching, roasting, and making soups. The

TIPS FOR SUCCESS

• When steaming potentially sticky foods such as wontons, line plate with lettuce and place wontons on top. The dumplings will not stick to the lettuce and clean up is easy. Please remember to compost the lettuce.

Chinese designed them as an all-purpose pot. If I had to choose only one pot for my kitchen, it would be an easy choice: a great wok!

• **Non-stick woks** may seem like a good choice; they are light in weight and easy to clean, but most cannot take the high heat required for stir-frying. Also, some studies are finding that the non-stick coating may be a health risk. Other types of woks, when seasoned properly will become naturally non-stick.

• **Stainless steel woks** look shiny and beautiful, but I would not recommend one. My first stir-fry pan was a copper exterior with a stainless-steel interior, both great cooking materials. I used it for years and thought it was fine. The reason I replaced it was because it became too small as my family's appetite grew. After I purchased a traditional wok, I realized there was a world of difference in the finished food; I have

not used my stainless wok since! Foods tend to stick more on stainless because it cannot be seasoned. They are usually more expensive, heavier, and do not conduct heat as well.

• **Cast iron woks** have been around for centuries and are very durable. When properly maintained, they can last decades. They take longer to heat and cool, but they hold heat well and heat more evenly over other types of materials. They also produce a better non-stick surface when seasoned.

• **A carbon steel wok is my material of choice!** They are lightweight, inexpensive, heat very quickly, cool very quickly, and season to a non-stick nicely. They have also been around for centuries, and chefs are tied on which is better, carbon steel or cast iron. I went with the carbon steel over the cast iron because of the weight difference, but both are a great choice. I absolutely love my wok!

• **Round bottom vs. flat bottom:** Round bottoms are traditional and a better choice. However, they are not as stable, and you will need to purchase a wok ring to fit on your burner. Round bottoms are great with gas stove tops, and can be adapted to electric cook tops, but usually flat-bottomed woks are used instead on electric.

Seasoning is the process of using fats to create a unique non-stick coating on the cooking surface. Seasoning is important when using metals such as carbon steel or cast iron. These metals are porous, rust easily, and need to be seasoned. You must take care of your wok to maintain this finish but don't worry, it's easy. If for some reason the patina wears off, you can always re-season it. The more you use your wok, the better the seasoning will become. Also, it is best to remove the food immediately after

TIPS FOR SUCCESS

• Make sure all foods are prepped and within reach before you begin to stir-fry.

• The pieces should be smaller rather than larger and cut uniformly for even cooking.

• Do not overcrowd the wok! Working in a several smaller batches will yield greater results as opposed to cooking it all at once.

• Spread your meat in a single layer across the hot wok to produce a beautiful caramelized sear.

• Slightly undercook the first batch of vegetables and meat as it will continue to cook while it is sitting covered.

• If your meat seems to have a lot of liquid, use a slotted spoon to strain it before placing in the hot wok. You don't want the meat to boil, you want it to fry. The accumulated juices can be added after the meat is cooked so you still get the delicious flavors.

cooking and place in a pre-warmed serving dish, rather than letting the food and liquids sit in the wok. Wipe with paper towel until ready to clean.

Seasoning is easy, but a very important process! Your wok will most likely come with directions. If not, here are simple instructions:

Start by scrubbing it thoroughly with soap and hot water. Oils are used in the manufacturing process and need to be completely removed or they will leave behind a bad taste. Dry and place over high heat. Add a tablespoon or two of oil and swirl to coat. Be careful during this process. You want to "burn" the oil into your wok. It will eventually turn into a very dark patina. I also recommend adding sliced scallions and pieces of ginger to the process. Cook them until they are charred. This adds great flavor to your seasoning and removes any metallic taste.

Cleaning is a breeze; rinse under hot water and use a soft brush to remove any food or sauces. Do not use soap! Dry with paper towel and place over heat for a minute or so to be sure it is completely dry. When cool, rub surface with a light oil coating. It really is that easy!

Local chefs preparing picarones, Cieneguilla, Peru.

Habits

COMPOSTING IS AN IMPORTANT PART of cooking to me. I have done it since I was a child. It serves many purposes and is easy. It decreases the garbage in landfills, it is nature's recycling, and it makes great fertilizer for your yard.

I encourage everyone to start composting without any excuses. It can be as simple as digging a hole in your yard, to purchasing a compost bin at the local home store. There are even indoor composting systems for those living in city apartments! See, no excuses.

A few basic rules to composting: only use vegetable scraps or yard vegetation, no meat or oils because they take longer to break down and can attract scavenger animals.

Once you see how much your trash is reduced and the rich black soil that your scraps turn into, you will understand how important it is for our environment. Please make it a daily habit by having a collection container within reach at all times in the kitchen.

Warm plates enhance a great meal. I am sure you have noticed that I finish most recipes by instructing food to be served on a pre-warmed plate. If you are going to go to the work to prepare a nice meal, complete it in style! Who wants to eat cold food? Restaurants serve your meal with instructions, "Be careful, the plate is very hot," and you should too!

The little touches can set you apart and help you go from an ordinary cook to an extraordinary cook! If you have an extra oven, or are not using the oven, place it on

TIPS FOR SUCCESS

A great Peruvian cook always has on hand:
- Pisco
- Rice
- Potatoes
- Aji
- Garlic
- Ginger
- Onions
- Fresh Limes
- Pisco
- Rice
- Potatoes
- Peruvian Olives
- Hard Boiled Eggs
- Wok
- Chop Sticks
- Soy Sauce
- *Did I mention Pisco, rice, and potatoes?*

a low temperature (170-190 degrees F), and put your plates and serving dishes inside while you are cooking. Another option is to rinse them under hot water before serving. Some people swear by warming them in the microwave, but I have read mixed reviews on this. Please make sure your dishes are ovenproof and heat safe.

Helping others less fortunate is a gratifying habit we should all partake in. Most of us take for granted the mere fact that we were born in a prosperous country. The majority of the world is not so fortunate. I encourage you to "Pay it forward" and help others less privileged. That doesn't mean that you have to run out and sign up for a mission trip half-way around the world; you can simply volunteer in your local community. In fact, you have already done a small part by purchasing *Family Secrets*. A portion of the proceeds will go towards the Peruvian American Medical Society, a voluntary, nonprofit organization providing much needed medical care and health education to underserved populations in Peru since the 1970s. For more information, please visit their website: pamsweb.org.

Peru is home for my extended family, has educated my husband, has graced me with its beauty, and helped me discover a whole new world of flavors! I want to give back to this inspiring country!

Waiting to see the doctor.
Photo by David Moretz/Scire Design

Aragón family
"parrillada"

Coming together with family and friends at the table should be an essential part of life. It's a time to relax, talk, and share your secrets! The meals in this book are mostly everyday meals with the exceptions of a few; those should be saved for holidays and other special occasions. I suggest you host a Peruvian dinner fiesta, and I will help you with sample menus (see Menu Suggestions). As you get more comfortable, move on to some of the recipes that you may consider more challenging.

The most important step to enjoying a great meal is to be thankful for your food. Begin each meal with a prayer, and do not forget to thank God, and those who worked to grow and provide your food. Consuelo would literally spend hours cooking for my family. Yet each day, before excusing herself to clean the kitchen, she would always say, "Thank you Katie and Rogelio for dinner." It would leave me humbled.

Drinks

Chicha Morada
Café con Leche
Té Helado a la Consuelo
Inca Kola
Pisco Sour

The green cliffs of Miraflores, Peru, also known as the Costa Verde.

Chicha Morada

Purple Corn Drink

The Andean Cultures have enjoyed the benefits of purple corn for millennia, and it is time we do too! This is a truly refreshing and distinctive beverage packed full of antioxidants the whole family will enjoy. Mix it with sparkling water for a gourmet soda taste.

INGREDIENTS

12 cups of water

1 (15 ounce) bag maiz morado
(dried purple Peruvian corn)

1 cinnamon stick

15 whole cloves

1 apple and 1 pineapple
(optional, see Tips for Success)

1¼ cups granulated sugar

½ cup lime juice, freshly squeezed

4 cups or more ice cubes

Sparkling water
(optional, see Tips for Success)

SERVES

16 (8 ounce servings)

Bring water, corn, cinnamon, cloves, and apple rind and pineapple rind (if using) to a boil in a large pot, covered, over high heat. Reduce heat, and simmer 30 minutes.

Cool to room temperature and strain liquid into large pitcher. Remove and compost solids.

Add sugar, lime juice, and apple and pineapple chunks (if using). Stir well and add enough ice to equal 1 gallon. Refrigerate.

Serve well-chilled.

TIPS FOR SUCCESS

• Another nice variation to this recipe is to add pineapple rind and apple rind to the pot of water when simmering. Once strained and cooled, add small chunks of fresh pineapple and apple to pitcher to give it a sangria look, without the alcohol.

• For those of you who can't live without carbonated beverages, mix this with sparkling water just before serving to satisfy your craving for fizz. It's surprisingly refreshing!

Café con Leche

Coffee with Milk

Café con leche was a staple in the Choy household. My husband distinctly remembers his mother at the stove percolating a pot of very strong coffee and boiling a pan full of milk. They enjoyed a cup with breakfast and another one in the afternoon each day. Although I am not a coffee drinker, I do enjoy a hot cup of café con leche!

INGREDIENTS

3 ounces espresso or very strong coffee, hot and fresh

5 ounces whole milk, scalded

Lots of sugar

SERVES

Single 8 ounce serving

Combine the espresso/coffee with the hot milk. Stir in sugar, as much as you like.

Serve with breakfast or anytime throughout the day as they do in Peru.

TIPS FOR SUCCESS
• For a great tasting café con leche, be sure to use strong, high quality coffee beans along with good tasting water.

Peru is the 8th largest producer of coffee in the world, and is the 5th largest producer of the Arabica bean.

ABOVE: Famous for its sad tale, you can watch the reenactment of the diving priest from this beautiful seaside restaurant, El Salto del Fraile, Chorrillos, Peru.

LEFT: Beautiful Pacific wave patterns, Miraflores, Peru.

Té Helado a la Consuelo

Consuelo's Iced Tea

This is a delicious blend of iced tea and limeade (very similar to an "Arnold Palmer" that we enjoy here in the U.S.A.). I use freshly squeezed Key limes from my tree, but regular limes or lemons are just as refreshing. When friends would visit while Consuelo was here, she always served them her iced tea, and it left a lasting impression. They still ask for her recipe!

INGREDIENTS

14 cups cold water, divided

3 tea bags

1 ¼ cups granulated sugar

½-¾ cup lime juice, freshly squeezed (see Tips for Success)

2 cups ice cubes

SERVES

16 (8 ounce servings)

Pour 2 cups water in small saucepan, bring to boil, and add tea bags. Remove from heat and let steep 15 minutes.

Remove tea bags. Stir in sugar while still warm. Pour into a one gallon pitcher and stir in lime juice, 12 cups cold water, and ice cubes.

Serve well-chilled.

TIPS FOR SUCCESS

• Ripe yellow Key limes can be much more tart than Persian limes, so if you are using Key limes, ½ cup of juice is sufficient; otherwise you may prefer ¾ cup juice.

Peru has 1625 types of orchids, of which 425 can be found growing naturally close to Machu Picchu. The Inkaterra Hotel in Machu Picchu has South America's largest privately owned collection at 500 varieties.

Inca Kola

The Golden Kola

Peru's national soda, Inca Kola, is a very sweet soda made from lemon verbena with a unique golden color. To me, it has a bubble gum/cream soda flavor. My kids love it, and it is a fun addition to a Peruvian meal!

INGREDIENTS

1 bottle or can of Inca Kola, well chilled

SERVES

Single 8 ounce serving

Serve cold and refreshing straight from the bottle!

TIPS FOR SUCCESS

• Inca Kola is great mixed with various liquors, such as Pisco, light rum, or vodka for a beautiful golden cocktail. Top it off with a squeeze of lime and a maraschino cherry to give it the perfect touch.

Inca Kola is the leading bottled beverage sold in Peru. For years, Coca-Cola and Pepsi tried to dominate the Peruvian market, but despite their vast resources, they were never able to overtake Inca Kola as the preferred soft drink of the Peruvian public.

Pisco Sour

An Absolute Must with Every Peruvian Meal!

The first thing everyone asks is, "What exactly is Pisco?" The easiest answer is, "Peruvian moonshine!" Pisco is made by fermenting and distilling grapes, and it has a very high alcohol content. Beware, a Pisco Sour goes down very smoothly, but believe me, one is enough!

INGREDIENTS

6 ounces of Pisco

2 ounces simple syrup

2 ounces lime juice, freshly squeezed

1 cup ice cubes

1 egg white

Angostura Bitters

SERVES

4 (8 ounce servings)

Place the first 4 ingredients in a blender and blend on high until smooth. Add egg white and blend another 30 seconds until foamy.

Pour into glass and top with a drop or two of Angostura bitters.

Serve with friends, "Salud!"

TIPS FOR SUCCESS

• Make sure you purchase a Peruvian brand of Pisco—it's way better.

• Simple syrup can be made ahead of time and stored in refrigerator for quick use. It is a ratio of 1 part water to 2 parts sugar. Bring water to a boil and stir in sugar until completely dissolved. Remove from heat and let cool.

• If using Key limes in this recipe, it requires a bit more simple syrup due to their higher acidity content.

The Pisco Sour is Peru's national drink and is made using Pisco brandy, lemons, sugar water, egg whites, ice and finished with bitters.

LEFT: My brother-in-law, Edi Choy serving Pisco Sours.

BELOW: Edi, Consuelo, and Rogelio celebrating her 90th; all she wanted was a margarita for her birthday!

Salads

Ensalada a la Consuelo

Ensalada de Huevo
a la Consuelo

Ensalada de Vainita
y Zanahoria

Causa Rellena

Nabo Encurtido

Local produce market, Lince District of Lima, Peru. My father-in-law, Pancho, ran his poultry store in this very same market for many years.

Outskirts of Lima, Peru.

Ensalada a la Consuelo

Consuelo's Salad

Consuelo is always looking for something to do or something to prepare. This simple yet deliciously refreshing salad was created on one of those days.

INGREDIENTS

2 apples, diced

2 stalks celery, diced

1 large carrot, grated

1 bell pepper, diced

⅓ cup sweet or red onion, minced

½ cup pecans, roughly chopped

½ cup raisins

3-4 tablespoons mayonnaise

Juice from 1 lime

Salt and pepper, to taste

3-4 lettuce leaves, washed and dried

Stir together all ingredients except lettuce, cover and chill.

Serve over bed of lettuce.

TIPS FOR SUCCESS

• To give this salad a really a beautiful presentation, be sure to use red apples and brightly colored bell peppers.

SERVES: 4-6

Ensalada de Huevo a la Consuelo

Consuelo's Egg Salad

I would guess as you came to this recipe you may have thought to yourself, egg salad? I know how to make egg salad. Why is it in this collection? That's because you probably haven't had egg salad the way Consuelo makes it, with freshly squeezed lime juice. My daughter had a few friends over one day and I had to come up with a quick lunch. I made this for them and they loved it. They told my daughter it was the best egg salad they ever had; I agree!

INGREDIENTS

12 eggs

3-4 generous tablespoons of mayonnaise

1 tablespoon fresh lime juice

Salt and pepper, to taste

3-4 lettuce leaves, washed and dried

A loaf of good sandwich bread (optional)

SERVES: 4-6

TIPS FOR SUCCESS

• Add slivered almonds, diced sweet onion, diced peppers, diced celery, raisins, or whatever you like to the egg salad.

Place eggs in medium size saucepan, cover with water, and turn heat to high. When water comes to a boil, reduce heat to maintain a gentle boil for 9 minutes.

Drain hot water, and while eggs are still in pan, gently shake to lightly crack the shells (this technique makes the eggs easier to peel by allowing water to seep in between membrane and egg). Immediately immerse in an ice water bath to cool for at least 10-15 minutes.

Peel eggs, dice, and toss into a large mixing bowl. Fold in mayonnaise, lime juice, salt and pepper. Taste and adjust seasonings.

Line serving platter with a bed of lettuce and spoon egg salad on top.

Serve alone or with bread (if using).

Ensalada de Vainita y Zanahoria

Green Bean and Carrot Salad

This salad sports a nice crunch, is easy to make, and can be adapted to almost any vegetable you prefer. Broccoli is especially delicious prepared this way.

INGREDIENTS

2 cups fresh green beans
(about ½ pound), sliced
on bias to 1 inch pieces

2 cups carrots, quartered
and diced

½ teaspoon salt, plus
more to taste

1 tablespoon vegetable oil

Juice from 1-2 limes

SERVES: 4-6

In a medium saucepan over high heat, bring the beans, carrots, ½ teaspoon salt, and 1 cup water to a boil. Reduce heat and maintain a simmer.

Cook about 6-7 minutes until vegetables are crisp-tender. Drain and rinse immediately with very cold water, or place in ice water bath for 1 minute to prevent further cooking.

Drain well on paper towels and place in medium sized serving dish. Add salt to taste, oil, and lime juice. Toss well to combine.

Serve at room temperature or chilled.

TIPS FOR SUCCESS

• If you have any leftover vegetables from last night's dinner, they can easily be transformed into this salad. Remove from refrigerator and toss with lime juice and salt. Voilà—you now have tonight's salad!

There are not too many vegetarian choices in local restaurants, but you will find a brave new veggie world in Lima supermarkets.

Causa Rellena

Layered Potato and Chicken Salad

Causa comes from the Incas believing the potato was the "Giver of Life." This is a dish layered with creamy yellow potatoes and mouthwatering chicken salad. It is typically served as a lunch or as a very popular picnic food. The chicken can be replaced with tuna or shrimp (see Tips for Success).

INGREDIENTS

3 pounds Yukon gold potatoes

¼ cup aji amarillo paste

6-8 tablespoons fresh lime juice, divided

2 teaspoons salt, divided

2 tablespoons vegetable oil

2 split chicken breasts

½ red onion, thinly sliced

½ red onion, diced small

1 stalk of celery, diced small

2-3 tablespoons mayonnaise

Black pepper, to taste

3-4 lettuce leaves, washed and dried

3 hard boiled eggs, peeled and halved

Aceitunas (Peruvian olives)

SERVES: 4-6

FOR THE DOUGH:

Scrub the potatoes and place in large pot with enough cold water to cover. Bring to a gentle boil over high heat and reduce to medium-low. Simmer 20 minutes or until tender, remove and let cool.

Peel potatoes and put through potato ricer. Place in large mixing bowl and add aji amarillo paste, starting with small amount and add to taste. Mix in 2 Tbsp. lime juice, 1 tsp. salt, and oil. Mix and knead well with hands. Adjust seasonings to taste, set aside.

FOR THE CHICKEN SALAD:

While potatoes are cooking, boil or roast chicken until done. Once cool enough to handle, pull apart chicken by hand into small pieces and set aside. Discard skin and bones (this can be done a day ahead and kept refrigerated).

Place sliced onion in serving bowl and marinate with 2 Tbsp. lime juice and sprinkle of salt. Set aside as accompaniment to final dish.

The potato is originally from Peru, and there are over 3,000 different varieties. Proud Peruvians use the phrase *Soy mas Peruano que la papa.* (I am more Peruvian than the potato).

Causa, or potato dough, for Causa Rellena

Filling for Causa Rellena

Place diced onions and celery in medium sized bowl. Marinate with 2-3 Tbsp. lime juice and sprinkle of salt for at least 30 minutes. Drain and reserve marinade.

In large mixing bowl, stir together chicken with diced onions and celery, mayonnaise, salt and pepper to taste. Starting with a tablespoon at a time, add reserved lime juice to taste.

TO ASSEMBLE:

In a greased 8x8 serving dish, spread ½ potato dough for base layer. Next, spread the chicken salad over potato for second layer. Top with remaining potato dough and spread until smooth.

Serve at room temperature over a bed of lettuce and garnish with hard-boiled eggs, Peruvian olives, and marinated sliced onions.

TIPS FOR SUCCESS

• In place of the chicken, 2 large cans of drained tuna or 1 pound of small cooked shrimp can be substituted.

• Each layer of this recipe is wonderful by itself. The "causa," or potato dough can be served as a side dish or appetizer. The chicken salad also can stand alone. The secret flavor comes from the addition of lime juice. When you are short on time, skip the potatoes and enjoy this chicken salad on a sandwich.

• Another option is to assemble the causa rellena for rustic-like individual servings. Start by taking a handful of dough, shape and pat it like a hamburger and set it on a plate. Spoon chicken salad overtop, and make another potato patty. Place this second patty on top and gently press together. Serve with accompaniments.

• A layer of freshly sliced avacado is also a nice addition to the filling.

Lima was founded by Spanish conquistador Francisco Pizarro on January 18, 1535.

Pachacámac, Quechua for Creator of the World, is an archeological site 40 miles SE of Lima, Peru, in the valley of the Lurin River. Occupation began around 200 AD.

TIPS FOR SUCCESS

• As delicious as this salad is, keep in mind the radish belongs to the cabbage family and omits a malodorous gas. Suggestion: open jar outdoors before serving.

Nabo Encurtido

Pickled Radish

This is a wonderfully crunchy, sweet-and-sour side to any meal. Daikon radishes, a.k.a. Chinese radish or white radish, are very common in Asian cuisine due to their subtle flavor. They can also be cut in a shoestring manner and used as a condiment on any sandwich.

INGREDIENTS

1 small nabo (Daikon radish, about 1 pound), peeled and thinly sliced

1 carrot, thinly sliced

1 tablespoon salt

1 cup white vinegar

6 tablespoons granulated sugar

SERVES: 4-6

Place radish and carrots in a colander and sprinkle with salt, mix well with hands, and let drain 1 hour. Rinse very well in cold water to remove excess salt and drain.

In a glass bowl or jar, stir vinegar with sugar until dissolved. Add vegetables and make sure they are fully submerged in liquid. Cover with airtight seal and refrigerate at least 4 hours.

Serve well chilled.

Overlooking a bullring, a soccer field, and the Pacific Ocean from Temple of The Sun, Pachacámac Ruins.

Starters

Ceviche

Anticuchos de Corazón

Papa Rellena

Papa a la Huancaina

Ocopa con Papas

Rocoto Relleno

Empanadas

Wontons

Caldo de Pollo

Caldo de Pollo y Wontons

Sancochado

Miraflores Coast, Peru

Ceviche

Lime Marinated Fish

Peru is well known for its ceviche. Fresh fish and fresh lime juice is a must for this to be successful. The enzymes in the lime juice cook the fish, no heat required. The reserved juice is known as "Leche de Tigre" and is served alongside; it is believed to be a cure for hangovers!

Place fish, shrimp and scallops (if using) in a glass dish. Mix salt, pepper, garlic, lime juice, aji amarillo (if using), and ginger (if using), pour over fish and stir. Make sure fish is fully immersed! Top with sliced onion and gently press it into the liquid. Cover and refrigerate.

Let the fish "cook" in marinade 2 hours or until fish is opaque.

Arrange lettuce leaves on a serving platter. Place sweet potatoes and corn atop lettuce. Use slotted spoon to place ceviche alongside and sprinkle with cilantro.

Serve in chilled martini glasses with a shot of the reserved marinade, and you probably will want to save a shot or two for later if you are drinking Pisco Sours!

INGREDIENTS

1 pound fresh firm white fish, cut into ½ inch cubes

¼ pound small shrimp (peeled and deveined) or small scallops (optional)

1 teaspoon salt

Black pepper, to taste

2 cloves garlic, pressed

1 cup or more lime juice, freshly squeezed

1 tablespoon aji amarillo paste (optional)

2 teaspoons ginger, freshly grated (optional)

1 medium red onion, thinly sliced

3-4 leaves of lettuce, washed and dried

1-2 sweet potatoes, boiled, peeled, and sliced

Steamed choclo/corn on the cob

1 tablespoon cilantro, minced

SERVES: 4-6

TIPS FOR SUCCESS

• I cannot stress enough the importance of very fresh fish and freshly squeezed lime juice for this recipe. Bottled juice will not work well.

• Make sure you remove all bones, skin, and bloodline from fish before cutting.

• If you like a little spice with your ceviche the way many Peruvians do, be sure to use the aji paste while marinating. Another option is to make it without the aji, and serve it separately on the side to stir in as you please.

• The fish can also be cut into long thin strips sashimi style, rather than cubed.

Presidential Palace, Lima, Peru.

El Beso sculpture in the Love Park, Miraflores, Peru.

High rise cosmopolitan building, Miraflores, Peru.

High rise apartments, Miraflores, Peru.

Rooftop, Miraflores, Peru.

Miraflores combines traditional and trendy influences, one of the reasons for Miraflores special charm and flair. Old houses coexist with modern multi-story buildings, hotels, casinos and banks. You find traditional cafes and restaurants next to modern European style establishments or fast food chains, cultural institutions next to discos and bars.

Miraflores by night.

Anticuchos de Corazón

Grilled Beef Heart Kabobs

Anticuchos originate back to Inca times; it seems they enjoyed a good barbecue as much as we do! This is a very popular Peruvian dish found everywhere from restaurants to street vendors to backyard fiestas. The smoky flavor is unbelievably delicious, and the recipe can be used with a wide variety of other meats. Prepare this at your next barbecue, and watch your guests coming back for more!

INGREDIENTS

2½ pounds beef heart, cut into 1½ inch cubes or long thin strips (see Tips for Success)

1 cup red wine vinegar

2 teaspoons cumin

1 teaspoon salt

½ teaspoon black pepper

5 cloves garlic, pressed

1 tablespoon aji panca paste

¼ cup vegetable oil

2 sweet potatoes, boiled, peeled, and sliced

Steamed choclo/corn on the cob

SERVES: 4-6

Place meat in a large bowl or resealable bag. Stir together vinegar, cumin, salt, black pepper, garlic, aji panca, and oil. Pour over meat, refrigerate, and let marinate 24-48 hours.

Pre-heat grill to high. Remove meat from marinade and reserve liquid. Thread meat onto barbecue skewers and place on hot grill for 3-4 minutes. Brush meat with reserved marinade, turn, and continue grilling another 3-4 minutes or until medium, with a little pink inside. Discard unused marinade.

Serve immediately on warm plates, accompanied with choclo or corn on the cob and sweet potatoes.

TIPS FOR SUCCESS

• To keep meat from spinning on skewers when turning, thread them through two skewers rather than one.

• Depending on how the butcher cuts the meat, long thin strips work well too, rather than cubes and provides more surface area for the marinade.

• Anticuchos are great when dipped in Huancaina sauce (page 62) or Ocopa sauce (page 64).

Peru grows more than 55 varieties of corn, and you can find it in just about any color including yellow, purple, white, and black.

Papa Rellena

Meat Stuffed Potato

This traditional Peruvian dish is a bit more labor intensive, but definitely worth the work. The process becomes fun when everyone gets their hands in the dough! These are often served as an appetizer, but are hearty enough for a main meal. Consuelo would easily make 50 of these for her family of 5, and they would devour every one. These are my absolute favorite, and the meat is also scrumptious in Empanadas (page 69), Rocoto Relleno (page 67), and also makes a great taco filling.

INGREDIENTS

5 pounds (about 6 large) Idaho potatoes

5-6 large eggs, best at room temperature

1 quart vegetable oil, divided

1 medium onion, finely diced

2-3 tablespoons aji panca paste, depending on how hot you like it

4 teaspoons salt, divided

1 teaspoon cumin

½ teaspoon oregano

2 cloves garlic, pressed

1½ pounds ground beef

1 beef bouillon cube

²/₃ cup raisins

Flour for dusting

SERVES

Makes about 2 dozen

Place potatoes and 2 eggs in a large pot of water over high heat. Bring to boil, lower heat to maintain simmer, and set timer for 9 minutes. Remove eggs only and plunge in ice water bath. Continue to boil potatoes until soft, about another 20 minutes. Remove potatoes and set side to cool. Peel egg and dice, set aside to be used with meat filling.

While the potatoes are cooking, heat 1 Tbsp. oil in a large Dutch oven over medium-high heat. Cook onion for 3-4 minutes, stirring occasionally to prevent burning. Add aji panca, ½ teaspoon salt, cumin, and oregano and continue cooking another 3-4 minutes. Reduce heat to medium and add garlic, cook 1 minute.

Add ground beef and bouillon (this is where you can substitute cooked quinoa for the ground beef to make it vegetarian; see Tips for Success). Stir to break up meat and continue to cook until meat is brown and all flavors are incorporated. Stir in diced hard-boiled eggs and raisins. Cook 1-2 minutes more, cover and set aside. One batch yields approximately 4 cups and can be made a day ahead and kept refrigerated.

Heavily sprinkle counter with flour. When potatoes are cool enough to handle, peel and put through potato ricer onto floured countertop. Sprinkle with 3 tsp. salt and add 1

Potato dough for Papa Rellena

Filling for Papa Rellena

raw egg. With heavily floured hands, mix and knead potatoes to a smooth, dough-like consistency. If you feel it needs more egg, start by adding only an egg-white to keep dough from getting too wet.

The key step is to continually flour hands to keep dough from from sticking. Take about ¹/₃ cup of dough and press gently to flatten. Press into a cupped hand to make a well. Spoon 1 Tbsp. of meat into center. Carefully close dough around meat and shape into an oval, potato shaped form. Roll in flour and place on a floured or parchment lined baking sheet. Repeat with remaining dough. Any leftover meat should be refrigerated or frozen for another use, such as tacos, Empanadas (page 69), or Rocoto Relleno (page 67).

Fill deep fryer or pan with 2-3 inches of oil and heat to 375 degrees F. While oil is heating, beat 2 eggs in shallow dish. Take 1 filled potato

and dip into beaten egg and then very carefully place in hot oil, no more than 3 at a time. Fry until golden brown, about 2-3 minutes, gently turning halfway through cooking. Remove carefully from hot grease with spider strainer or slotted spoon. Place on paper towel lined plate and let cool several minutes.

Serve on platter and enjoy!

TIPS FOR SUCCESS

• Be sure not to overcook potatoes and remove promptly when done, otherwise they can absorb water. If the potatoes are too wet, the dough can be difficult to work with.

• For a vegetarian version, use 3 cups cooked quinoa to replace the ground beef when preparing the filling.

• Long cooking chop sticks work beautifully in this recipe to turn potatoes when frying.

• When finished, these can be kept warm in a 200 degree F. oven.

• Aceitunas (Peruvian olives) make a great savory accompaniment to compliment the sweetness of the raisins.

Parapente, otherwise known as paragliding, overlooking Peru's most well-known and visited lighthouse on the cliffs of Miraflores, Peru.

Papa a la Huancaina

Potatoes with Spicy Cheese Sauce

Once again the Peruvians have created another one of their signature sauces using Consuelo's favorite ingredients: onions, garlic, and aji. Of course it wouldn't be complete without potatoes, hard-boiled eggs, and Peruvian olives! This is an instant hit at parties because of its beautiful presentation and flavor. Guests are always asking me for the recipe before they leave.

INGREDIENTS

5-6 Yukon gold potatoes

3-4 large eggs

1-2 tablespoons vegetable oil

1 small onion, diced

1-2 tablespoons aji amarillo paste, depending on how hot you like it

Salt, to taste

2 cloves garlic, pressed

1 pound queso fresco or other fresh cheese

4-5 saltine crackers

½ teaspoon turmeric

1 (12 ounce) can evaporated milk

3-4 lettuce leaves washed and dried

Aceitunas (Peruvian olives)

Sprinkle of paprika

SERVES: 6-8

Place potatoes and eggs in a medium sized pot and cover with cold water. Place over high heat and bring to a gentle boil. Lower heat to maintain simmer and set timer for 9 minutes. Remove eggs only and plunge into ice water bath. Continue simmering potatoes another 12-15 minutes until tender. Remove potatoes and set aside to cool.

In a small sauté pan, heat 1 Tbsp. oil over medium heat. Add onions and sauté 2-3 minutes, stirring often. Add aji amarillo paste, and a sprinkle of salt and continue cooking until onions are soft, about 5 minutes. Add garlic and cook another minute, remove from heat and let cool to room temperature.

Place onion mixture in blender with cheese, crackers, turmeric, and ½ can of milk. Blend well until smooth and creamy, adding more milk and salt as needed. If it becomes too thin, you can thicken it with more crackers.

Peel and slice potatoes and eggs in halves or quarters.

Create a bed of lettuce leaves on serving platter. Arrange potatoes, olives, and eggs atop lettuce. Drizzle with cheese sauce and lightly dust with paprika.

Serve at room temperature with additional sauce alongside in serving bowl.

TIPS FOR SUCCESS

• I usually do not offer substitutions for aji, but I have used fresh jalapeños or other hot peppers when aji was not available. It is similar but not quite the same.

• This sauce is nice when warmed and served over hot pasta or baked potatoes.

• My son created a fabulous twist on deviled eggs: when preparing the filling for deviled eggs, omit the mayonnaise, and replace it with Huancaina sauce. Blend yolks and sauce until smooth, fill the eggs, and sprinkle with paprika.

• If you are in a pinch for time, this can be put together rather quickly using the following shortcut: omit the onions and sautéing; simply put the aji, garlic, cheese, crackers, turmeric, and milk in blender and puree until smooth and creamy.

• This sauce gets very thick and pasty when refrigerated. To serve, microwave or heat in sauce pan on low heat until warm, stirring occasionally to return to smooth consistency.

• To keep yolk from sticking to knife when slicing eggs, start by using a very thin knife and lightly oil the blade, or wipe blade in between slices.

Ocopa con Papas

Potatoes with Cheese Sauce

This was the first Peruvian sauce I ever tasted and loved it immediately. We serve it over everything. Consuelo would pack it frozen in her luggage in Peru and manage to talk her way through customs when arriving at the Miami airport. I asked her once why doesn't she prepare it at my house instead of sneaking it in through customs. She said because she was not able to get huacatay in the United States. At the time, I was unfamiliar with the spice and asked her what it was. She leaned over and whispered, "It's similar to marijuana!" I thought to myself, hmmm ... what is she feeding us? Upon doing a little research I found out that huacatay is in the marigold family, not marijuana! We still get a laugh over that one.

INGREDIENTS

4-5 Yukon gold potatoes

3-4 large eggs

1-2 tablespoons vegetable oil

4 cloves garlic, peeled

¼ cup peanuts or walnuts

1 medium onion, diced small

1-2 tablespoons aji amarillo paste, depending on how hot you like it

½ teaspoon salt

½ cup or more of water

1 pound queso blanco or other fresh cheese

2 tablespoons huacatay paste

3-4 lettuce leaves, washed and dried

Aceitunas (Peruvian olives)

Sprinkle of paprika

SERVES: 6-8

Place potatoes and eggs in a medium sized pot, cover with cold water, and bring to boil over high heat. Lower heat to maintain simmer and set timer for 9 minutes. Remove eggs only and plunge into ice water bath. Continue simmering potatoes another 12-15 minutes or until tender. Remove potatoes and set aside to cool.

In medium sauté pan, heat 1 Tbsp. oil over medium heat. Sauté garlic cloves 2-3 minutes until golden and fragrant, stirring frequently. Be careful not to let them burn, lowering heat if necessary. Remove with slotted spoon and set aside to cool.

Add nuts to already hot and oily pan, and roast over medium heat for several minutes until fragrant and golden. Caution, they can burn quickly. Remove with slotted spoon, and let cool with garlic.

Return already hot pan with oil to medium heat, add a little more oil if necessary, and stir in onion, aji amarillo paste, and salt. Cook until onions are soft, about 5-6 minutes stirring often. Remove from heat and cool to room temperature.

Place garlic, nuts, onion mixture, water, caso blanco, and huacatay in blender. Puree until smooth and creamy, adding more water, a little at a time as needed. This sauce becomes very thin when heated, and thickens as it cools.

Pour sauce into medium sauce pan. Cover and simmer over low heat for 20 minutes. Remove from heat and cool to room temperature.

Peel eggs and potatoes and slice in halves or quarters. Lay atop bed of lettuce along with olives, drizzle with sauce, and sprinkle with light dusting of paprika.

Serve with additional sauce alongside in serving bowl.

TIPS FOR SUCCESS

• This sauce can be made ahead of time and kept refrigerated or even frozen. It will become very thick and pasty when cooled, but don't be alarmed; once reheated, it thins quickly.

• To keep the egg yolk from sticking to your knife while slicing eggs, start by using a very thin knife and lightly oil the blade, or wipe blade in between slices.

Miraflores Park, Peru, viewed from a high-rise apartment.

Walls of Saqsawaman ruins, located on the Northern outskirts of Cuzco, Peru, a popular tourist spot when beginning the journey to Machu Picchu.

Rocoto Relleno

Stuffed Hot Pepper

I grew up loving American-style stuffed peppers full of ground beef and rice, covered in tomato sauce. The Andean region of Peru has their own version of stuffed peppers too; however, their unique chile may be difficult to find in the U.S. The rocoto chile looks harmless but has quite a kick to it! If you are unable to find rocotos, don't worry, Consuelo has adapted the Peruvian Rocoto Relleno to the American bell pepper (see Tips for Success).

INGREDIENTS

6 rocoto chiles, fresh, frozen, or jarred

2 tablespoons granulated sugar

1½ teaspoons salt, divided

3 cups Papa Rellena meat (page 59)

2 eggs

1 (12 ounce) can evaporated milk

6 ounces caso fresco or mozzarella cheese, sliced or shredded

SERVES: 4-6

TIPS FOR SUCCESS

• "Pimiento Rellenos a la Consuelo" a.k.a. Stuffed Bell Peppers, Consuelo Style: take 6 bell peppers and cut off tops and remove seeds. Blanch peppers and tops in salted boiling water for 3 minutes and remove. Drain and cool on paper towels. Continue with step 2 above. It may require up to 4 cups of meat depending on size of peppers. Serve and enjoy. (See page 18.)

• For a delicious vegetarian twist, use cooked quinoa in place of the ground beef when preparing the filling. (See Papa Rellena recipe's Tips for Success, page 60.)

Begin by donning disposable gloves. Cut tops off of rocotos and set aside, remove seeds and veins and discard. Sprinkle insides of chiles with sugar and let sit 5 minutes.

Fill a medium sized pot with water, place over high heat, and bring to a boil. Add 1 tsp. salt, submerge chiles, and boil for 3 minutes. Remove, drain well, and let cool. If you are using rocotos preserved in brine, you may skip this step.

Pre-heat oven to 350 degrees F.

Fill chiles with meat, but do not pack it tightly; leave space for the custard. Place in an ovenproof dish.

Whisk eggs with ½ teaspoon salt and evaporated milk. Pour over chiles, letting it run inside and around the them.

Top with cheese and replace lid of chile. Bake 20-25 minutes until hot and custard is set.

Serve on warm plates.

TIPS FOR SUCCESS

• The dough can also be made in a large food processor affixed with metal blade. Start by pulsing dry ingredients 2-3 times to mix. Next, cut in shortening by using 12-15 short pulses. Last, pour in ice water while running until it comes together in a large ball. Do not over mix or dough may become tough.

• For easy clean-up, line baking sheet with parchment paper to keep egg wash from sticking.

• To ensure a successful dough, be sure to use fresh, high-quality shortening and flour. These emapanadas are too delicious to have them ruined by rancid shortening or stale flour.

• I suggest using an adjustable pastry board when rolling the dough to ensure uniform thickness in each one.

Empanadas

Meat Pies

Empanadas are one of those special delights that everyone must try! The dough has a hint of sweetness coupled with the sweet and savory meat filling that makes for a fabulous treat. They can be served as an appetizer or are hearty enough for a main meal. Experiment with various fillings and get the whole family involved. They are as fun to make as they are to eat!

INGREDIENTS

5 cups all-purpose flour, plus more for rolling

2 teaspoons salt

6 tablespoons granulated sugar

1 ⅔ cups shortening, well-chilled

¾-1 cup ice water

4 cups meat filling: Papa Rellena meat (page 59) or Aji de Gallina meat (page106)

1 egg, at room temperature

1 tablespoon milk or half and half, at room temperature

SERVES

Makes about 2 dozen

In a large mixing bowl, combine flour, salt and sugar. Add shortening and cut in with pastry blender until crumbly. Sprinkle with ice water 1 Tbsp. at a time and stir with fork until mixture is moistened and comes together in a ball. Divide dough into 2 or 3 equal balls and press to a disc shape. Wrap in plastic and chill dough for 20-30 minutes.

Pre-heat oven to 450 degrees F.

Take a disc of dough and place on a floured surface. Flour rolling pin to prevent dough from sticking and roll to 1/8 inch thickness. Cut 4-5 inch wide circles (we found a large martini glass to be the perfect size). Fill each one with about 2 Tbsp. meat. Moisten edges with water and carefully fold over. Press with fork to seal. Place on an ungreased baking sheet. Repeat with all remaining dough.

Whisk together egg and milk/half and half to make glaze.

Brush empanadas with glaze, and bake 15-20 minutes or until golden brown. Let cool at least 10 minutes.

Serve on platter and devour!

TIPS FOR SUCCESS

• For a delicious vegetarian version, substitute cooked quinoa for the ground beef when preparing the filling. See Papa Rellena recipe's Tips for Success (page 60).

• When finished, these can be kept warm in a 200 degree F. oven.

Wontons

Chinese Dumplings

Watching Consuelo fold wontons with such ease is an art in itself! When she is finished, the tray looks as if it is filled with traditional mitre caps. I prefer the much easier 4-corner method of folding wontons! We enjoy wontons steamed, fried, or in soup (page 75).

INGREDIENTS

1 pound ground pork

1-2 teaspoons ginger, grated

1-2 teaspoons sesame oil

1-2 green onions, thinly sliced

2-3 tablespoons soy sauce

Black pepper, to taste

1 package wonton wrappers

SERVES

Makes about 3 dozen

In a large bowl, gently mix together pork, ginger, sesame oil, green onions, soy sauce, and black pepper.

Place about 1 generous teaspoon of meat in center of wonton wrapper. Moisten edges with water and fold in preferred manner, press to seal. Place on cookie sheet, cover with plastic wrap, and refrigerate until ready to use.

Cook as desired: deep fry, steam, or boil in soup (page 75). See Tips for Success.

Serve as desired.

TIPS FOR SUCCESS

• To deep fry: Heat 1 quart vegetable oil in a deep fryer or large pan to 360 degrees F. Carefully place 4-5 wontons in hot oil and fry 3-5 minutes until golden, turning halfway through. Remove with spider strainer and place on paper towel lined plate. Cut one in half to be sure meat is cooked through. Repeat with remaining wontons.

• To steam: Line plate or steamer basket with cabbage or lettuce leaves. Place wontons on top and leave space in between to allow steam to bathe wontons. Place in steamer, cover and steam 8-10 minutes or until meat is no longer pink in center. Serve immediately with soy sauce.

• Be sure not to overfill wontons to keep meat from leaking out during cooking.

• If you have leftover meat, shape into small meatballs and add to boiling chicken broth or wonton soup. Cook 3-5 minutes or until no longer pink in center.

The National University of San Marcos is the oldest in the Americas and was founded on the 12th of May of 1551. My husband, Rogelio, is a graduate of San Marcos University Medical School.

Caldo de Pollo

Chicken Broth

Especially great for nursing mothers or for an upset stomach, ginger is believed to have soothing properties. This broth is clean and crisp, a perfect base for a variety of soups. Consuelo prepared this for me each time I brought a baby home from the hospital!

INGREDIENTS

1 large chicken, cut into parts, skin and fat removed and discarded

3 inch piece of ginger root, peeled and cut into thirds

12 cups water

1 tablespoon salt

SERVES: 4-6

Place all ingredients into a large stock pot and cover. Place over high heat and bring to a gentle boil, reduce heat to maintain a simmer for 3-4 hours, occasionally skimming and discarding foam that accumulates on surface.

Strain broth and pull chicken meat from bones, discarding ginger and bones. Place meat in serving bowl, cover, and keep warm.

Serve steaming hot with meat passed separately.

TIPS FOR SUCCESS

• I like to use my pasta pot when making soup. Once it is done, I simply lift out the strainer insert with all of the solids and I am left with a pot full of broth. I find it much easier and safer than trying to pour and strain the hot broth.

• Broth can be made up to 3 days ahead and refrigerated. Once chilled, any remaining grease turns to a white solid on the surface and is easy to remove and discard.

• This broth and chicken makes a great base for noodle soup, vegetable soup, wonton soup, etc.

The enormous Inca Empire was centered around the Andes Mountain range, the civilization's capital city of Cuzco, and mountaintop citadel Machu Picchu, all of which are extremely popular with visitors to this day.

Soaring like condors over the Miraflores coast, which is known as one of the best places in the world for parapente.

Caldo de Pollo y Wontons

Wonton Soup

As a child, I looked forward to our traditional German style chicken noodle soup on Sundays, with a big squirt of Heinz ketchup stirred into the bowl! I also fell in love with Consuelo's Asian twist on chicken soup with the infusion of ginger and wontons. It warms your heart and soul!

INGREDIENTS

8-10 cups Caldo de Pollo (page 73)

3-4 stalks bok choy, leafy part and stalk separated and sliced

3-4 nappa leaves, leafy part and stalk separated and sliced

16-20 uncooked Wontons (page 71)

1 green onion, thinly sliced

SERVES: 4-6

In a large stock pot over high heat, bring Caldo de Pollo to a boil, and add bok choy stalk and nappa stalk. Reduce heat, cover and simmer 5 minutes.

Add leafy portions of bok choy and nappa, along with wontons and continue to simmer another 4-5 minutes, or until meat is no longer pink.

Serve piping hot topped with green onion.

TIPS FOR SUCCESS

• If you have any leftover pork mixture, now is a good time to use it. Roll into small meatballs and add to boiling broth along with wontons.

• If you saved the chicken from preparing the broth, tear into bite size pieces and add to cooked soup.

Sancochado

Beef Vegetable Soup

Deliciously satisfying beef vegetable soup is so filling, you won't need anything else except another bowl! This is by far my husband's favorite soup. This is served in a de-constructed manner where the vegetables and beef are served separately from the broth so you can customize and choose exactly what you want in your bowl.

INGREDIENTS

8 cups water

2 pounds beef shank or ribs

1 stalk celery, halved

2 carrots, peeled and cut into thirds

1 large onion, halved

1 tablespoon salt

1 small yucca, peeled, halved, and cut into large pieces

3 small potatoes, scrubbed and halved

1 large wedge of cabbage (about ½ pound)

2 ears of choclo or 2 ears of corn, cut into thirds

Hot rice

SERVES: 4-6

Place water, beef, celery, carrots, onion, and salt in a large stock pot and bring to a gentle boil over high heat. Skim and discard any foam that accumulates. Cover, reduce heat, and simmer 3-4 hours.

Strain broth and place vegetables in covered serving bowl to keep warm. Slice meat into large pieces, discarding bone and fat. Cover to keep warm. Skim and discard excess grease from broth.

Return broth to pot and bring to a boil. Add yucca, potatoes, cabbage and choclo/corn. Cover, lower heat, and simmer 20 minutes or until vegetables are tender. Remove vegetables and place in serving bowl.

Serve steaming hot soup broth in individual bowls. Pass around meat, vegetables, and rice with serving spoons to add to hot broth as desired.

TIPS FOR SUCCESS

• If you prefer a more intense beef flavor, sear the meat in hot oil until brown and caramelized prior to adding the water. Use a spoon to scrape any brown bits and deglaze the pan. Continue with recipe.

• I like to remove the fibrous tissue from center of yucca before cooking by cutting a small wedge down the center.

• Broth can be made up to 3 days ahead and refrigerated. Once chilled, the fat turns to a white solid on the surface and is easy to remove and discard.

The capital city of Peru is Lima, which is home to more than a quarter of Peru's population.

Sides

Arroz Amarillo

Puré de Papa a la Consuelo

Frijoles con Arroz

Tallarines Verdes

Huevos al Vapor

Vast panoramic view of Cuzco, Peru, the ancient capital city of the Inca Empire, from the Saqsawaman ruins.

Arroz Amarillo

Yellow Rice

Yellow rice is a beautiful way to brighten up any meal. It is very easy to prepare, yet looks so impressive!

INGREDIENTS

3 tablespoons vegetable oil

¼ cup carrot, finely grated

½ teaspoon turmeric

1½ teaspoons salt

2 cups long grain rice

4 cups water (see Tips for Success)

1 cup frozen peas

1 cup frozen corn

1 cup frozen carrots

2 chicken bouillon cubes

SERVES: 4-6

Heat oil in a medium size pan over medium-high heat, add grated carrots, turmeric, and salt. Cook and stir 1 minute, and then add rice and cook and stir for 1 minute more. Add water, peas, corn, carrots, and bouillon and stir well to mix.

Bring to boil, cover, and reduce heat to simmer for 20 minutes or until rice is tender and all water is absorbed.

Serve alongside favorite meal on warm plates.

TIPS FOR SUCCESS

• Always check your rice directions for the water-to-rice ratio and adjust if necessary. My recipe is based on a 2:1 ratio.

• If you are in a pinch for time, go ahead and skip the grated carrots; their sole purpose is to add extra color. Don't worry, it will still be beautiful, only a little less bright.

My two boys, Armand and Stefan, meeting with
local Quechua people and llama, Cuzco, Peru.

Native Quechua people with their livestock, Cuzco, Peru.

Puré de Papa a la Consuelo

Consuelo's Mashed Potatoes

Consuelo whips these until they are extra smooth and creamy, the way mashed potatoes are supposed to be! I always make these with Consuelo's roast pork recipe (page 89); they are a pair made in heaven!

INGREDIENTS

2½ pounds Yukon gold or red creamer potatoes

2½ teaspoons salt, divided

1 stick unsalted butter, at room temperature

½-¾ cup half-and-half, warmed

⅓ cup sour cream

Black pepper, to taste

½ cup sharp cheddar cheese, grated (optional)

SERVES: 4-6

Peel, dice, and place potatoes in a medium size pot with enough water to cover. Add 1 tsp. salt to water and bring to a gentle boil over high heat. Reduce heat, cover and simmer for 20 minutes, or until tender. Drain well and place in mixing bowl. If making gravy, reserve ½-¾ cup potato water (see page 89).

Using an electric mixer with the whisk attachment, add butter to potatoes and whip until blended. Add half-and-half a little at a time, sour cream, 1tsp. salt, black pepper, and cheese (if using). Whip on high speed until very smooth and creamy, adding a little more half-and-half and salt if necessary. The key is to whip them long enough to be smooth and use enough liquid to keep them from being pasty.

Serve on warm plate alongside your favorite dish.

Frijoles con Arroz

Beans and Rice

Don't think all beans and rice are the same; Peruvian aji adds the special touch to make this stand out from the others! Many people serve beans and rice as a side dish, but in our house it is a meal. This photo shows black beans, but you can choose your favorite type of bean. Try various types of sausages, or omit the meat altogether for a vegetarian version.

INGREDIENTS

1 pound dried beans, pre-soaked and drained, or 1 (28 ounce) can of beans, undrained

1-2 teaspoons salt, divided

2 bay leaves

2-3 tablespoons olive or vegetable oil, divided

1 small onion, diced

1 small bell pepper, diced

½ pound favorite sausage, or 3-4 slices of bacon, cut to 1 inch pieces

1 tablespoon aji panca paste

3 cloves garlic, pressed

½ teaspoon cumin

½ teaspoon dried oregano

3 tablespoons red wine vinegar

Hot rice

¼ cup cilantro, chopped

Sour cream

Avocado, sliced and sprinkled with lime juice and salt

Place pre-soaked beans, 1 tsp. salt, bay leaves, and 6-8 cups water in large pot over high heat, bring to boil, reduce heat. Cover and simmer 1½-2 hours until beans are tender, but not falling apart. Check beans often to prevent over cooking and turning mushy. Drain and reserve water. Omit this step if using canned beans.

In a large sauce pan, heat 2 Tbsp. oil over medium-high heat, add onions, pepper, and meat. Stir and cook for 3-4 minutes. Add aji panca, 1 teaspoon salt, garlic, cumin, and oregano and continue cooking 5-6 minutes until vegetables are tender, stirring often.

Gently stir in beans, 1 cup reserved water (or can beans, if using), and vinegar. Cover, lower heat, and simmer 30 minutes to let flavors infuse. Taste to adjust seasonings, add more reserved water or drizzle with a little oil if it seems too thick. Remove bay leaves.

Serve over hot rice on warm plates, top with cilantro, sour cream, and avocado.

SERVES: 4-6

Tallarines Verdes

Pasta with Peruvian Style Pesto

Tallarines Verdes is a perfect example of the world's transformation of foods. Italian pesto made its way across the ocean to the Peruvians, and they redefined it into their own creamy green sauce. This is a common side dish in Peru and is often served with fried steak or chicken Milanese and topped with a fried egg.

INGREDIENTS

1 pound favorite pasta noodles

4 cups fresh spinach
(about 6 ounces)

1 cup fresh basil leaves
(about ½ ounce)

¼ cup water

¼ teaspoon salt

8 ounces queso fresco cheese

2 cloves garlic

1 tablespoon vegetable oil

½ cup evaporated milk

Grated Parmesan cheese

SERVES: 4-6

Cook pasta according to package directions and drain.

While pasta is cooking, place spinach, basil, water, salt, cheese, and garlic in blender. Purée on high until smooth and creamy, stopping once or twice to scrape down the sides.

Heat oil in a large saucepan over medium heat, add contents of blender, stirring occasionally until hot, stir in evaporated milk.

Pour sauce over pasta and toss until coated.

Serve on warm plates and top with Parmesan cheese.

TIPS FOR SUCCESS
• If you want to "heat" this up a bit, sauté 1 small diced onion and a tablespoon or two of aji Amarillo in a little hot oil until onions are soft. Cool 10 minutes and add to blender with other ingredients.

Cuzco, Peru was the most important city in the whole of the Inca Empire and governed as far north as Quito, Ecuador and Santiago, Chile.

Urubamba River and The Sacred Valley,
near Cuzco, Peru.

Huevos al Vapor

Steamed Eggs

Pancho loved his native Cantonese dishes and the splendor of Asian flavors. Steamed eggs can be traced back to the rural villages in the Canton Province and were thought of as a peasant dish. They are easy to prepare, inexpensive, but deliciously smooth and rich. My husband has warm memories of his father preparing this custard treat!

INGREDIENTS

10 large eggs

2 cups water

1 teaspoon salt

Soy sauce

4 green onions, thinly sliced

1 tablespoon dried shrimp, soaked in warm water for 20 min. (optional)

Oyster sauce (optional)

SERVES: 4-6

In a large heat-proof mixing bowl, whisk eggs, water, and salt. Can also be poured into individual ramekins.

Place bowl in steamer, cover, and steam 6-8 minutes (3-4 minutes for ramekins) until partially firm. Sprinkle with soy sauce, green onions, and shrimp (if using). Return to steamer and continue steaming until eggs are set.

Serve immediately with additional green onions and soy sauce or oyster sauce (if using).

Main Dishes

Asado de Cerdo

Pescado al Horno

Pescado al Vapor

Escabeche de Pollo

Arroz con Pollo

Pollo con Hongos

Arroz Chaufa

"Paticay"

Aji de Gallina

Saltado de Pollo
con Vegetales

Saltado de Nappa

Pollo Saltado

Saltado de Pollo
con Piña

Lomo Saltado

Saltado de Vainitas
con Papas Fritas

Saltado de Coliflor

Saltado de Carne
con Foo Gwa

Estofado de Carne

Estofado de Lengua

Estofado de Nabo

Tallarines Criollos

Carne al Vapor

Pasta al la Consuelo

Astonishing ancient engineering of the Inca wonder, Machu Picchu, Peru.

Asado de Cerdo

Roasted Pork

This is my favorite way to have pork: tender, juicy, and bursting with a kaleidoscope of flavors! The marinade makes plenty of drippings for the mouth-watering gravy to serve over the pork and creamy mashed potatoes, "Consuelo style" (see page 81).

INGREDIENTS

1 pork tenderloin, or any favorite cut of pork

3-4 tablespoons aji panca paste, depending on how hot you like it

5 cloves garlic, pressed

1 teaspoon cumin

½ cup red wine vinegar

1 teaspoon salt

Black pepper, to taste

Mashed potatoes (page 81) and ½ cup reserved potato water

2 tablespoons potato or corn starch whisked into ¼ cup cold water

SERVES: 4-6

Place pork in a large resealable bag. Mix aji panca, garlic, cumin, vinegar, salt, and pepper and pour over pork. Refrigerate and let marinate 1-4 hours.

Pre-heat oven to 350 degrees F. Place pork and marinade in an oven-proof dish and roast until tender and juicy with a meat thermometer registering 145 degrees F. Remove from oven, drain and reserve drippings. Cover pork with foil and allow to rest 10 minutes (temperature will continue to increase).

Gravy can be prepared while pork is resting by combining drippings with reserved potato water in medium saucepan over high heat. Bring to boil and whisk in starch mixture stirring constantly until thickened. Remove from heat and pour into gravy boat. Slice pork and place on warm platter.

Serve with mashed potatoes on warm plates and top with the decadent gravy.

TIPS FOR SUCCESS

• The key to tender, delicious pork is to not overcook it. In the past, we were taught to always cook pork to an internal temperature of 160 degrees F., thus resulting in over-cooked, dry pork. Recently, the FDA updated their guidelines deeming it safe and allowing an internal temperature of 145 degrees F., as long as you allow it to rest at least 3 minutes. Finally the FDA has allowed us to achieve what great chefs have known for years.

My husband, Rogelio, and my son, Stefan, hiking the much smaller, yet more difficult and dangerous mountain adjacent to Machu Picchu, Peru.

Machu Picchu, Peru

Views of Machu Picchu, Peru

Pescado al Horno

Baked Fish

For those of you afraid to cook fish, try this fool-proof method! This is very easy, healthy, and bursting with Asian flavor. Use the drippings to pour over the rice.

INGREDIENTS

2 pounds of favorite fish

2 teaspoons ginger, grated

5 tablespoons soy sauce

2 tablespoons vegetable oil

2 tablespoons water

1 tablespoon black bean sauce with garlic (optional)

4 green onions, thinly sliced

Hot rice

SERVES: 4-6

Pre-heat oven to 350 degrees F.

Rinse fish, pat dry, and place in baking dish. In a small bowl, combine ginger, soy sauce, oil, water, and black bean sauce (if using) and pour over fish, lifting with fork to allow some to run underneath.

Place in oven and bake 20-30 minutes or until fish is tender and flakes easily with a fork. Sprinkle with green onions and bake 1-2 minutes more.

Serve immediately with rice on warm plates, spooning juices overtop.

Pescado al Vapor

Steamed Fish

Steamed fish is light, delicate, and full of flavors. My husband remembers his childhood dinners where the plate of fish would be in the center of the table, and everyone would lean forward with their chopsticks to grab a bite! This recipe is not as accurate as I would like it to be. Unfortunately, my father-in-law passed away many years ago, and my husband and Consuelo do not remember exactly how he made it. This is our version ...

INGREDIENTS

4 green onions, whole

1 large or 2 small whole fish, cleaned and descaled

1 tablespoon ginger, grated or cut into tiny matchsticks

3 tablespoons soy sauce

1 tablespoon black bean sauce with garlic

1 tablespoon vegetable oil

1 tablespoon cilantro, chopped

2 green onions, thinly sliced

1 tablespoon potato or corn starch whisked into ¼ cup cold water

Hot rice

SERVES: 4-6

On a heat-proof dish or plate, place whole green onions in a grid pattern and lay fish overtop.

Stir together ginger, soy sauce, black bean sauce, and oil and pour over fish. Place in steamer, making sure the water level is below the dish.

Cover and gently steam 15-20 minutes or until eyes are opaque and meat flakes easily with fork.

Remove fish from steamer and drain accumulated juices into a small saucepan. Sprinkle fish with cilantro and sliced green onions. Cover to keep warm.

Heat saucepan with juices over medium-high heat until it begins to boil. Stir in starch mixture, continue stirring and cooking until sauce thickens. Pour over fish.

Serve immediately with chopsticks and rice on warm plates. Be careful of bones.

In the Peruvian ocean you can find over 700 fish species and 400 crustaceans. You will also find 20 out of 67 species of whales.

Escabeche de Pollo

Vinegar Marinated Chicken

What makes this dish so mouthwatering are the amazing flavors and textures. Serve this over rice to act as a sponge to absorb the marinade made of aji and a hint of vinegar. The crunch and sweetness of the onions compels your tongue back for seconds! This meal is typically served at room temperature, to allow time for the chicken to marinate in the sauce.

INGREDIENTS

10-12 skinless chicken thighs (or any chicken parts you prefer)

1 teaspoon salt, divided

2 large sweet onions, cut into ½ inch strips (see Tips for Success)

Black pepper, to taste

½ teaspoon cumin

¼ cup red wine vinegar

1 tablespoon vegetable oil

1-2 tablespoons aji panca paste, depending on how hot you like it

2 cloves garlic, pressed

Hot rice

SERVES: 4-6

Sprinkle chicken pieces with ½ tsp. salt. Place in a medium size pot with 1 cup water. Bring to boil, cover, reduce heat and simmer 20-30 minutes or until chicken is no longer pink. Remove from pot, reserve liquid, cover chicken and keep warm.

While chicken is cooking, spread onions in a dish and sprinkle with ½ teaspoon salt, pepper, cumin, and vinegar. Stir to coat, set aside to marinate.

In a large pot, heat oil over medium-high heat, add aji panca, and garlic. Cook 1 minute, stirring constantly. Add onions along with marinade and cook 3-4 minutes. Add 1 cup reserved liquid, cover, reduce heat, and simmer 5 minutes. Onions should be tender-crisp. Taste to adjust seasonings and add more broth if needed to balance vinegar.

Return chicken to pot, stir to coat well with sauce, cook 1 minute more. Remove from heat and let chicken marinate 30 minutes or longer.

Serve over hot rice on warm plates, spooning the onions and juice on-top.

TIPS FOR SUCCESS

• To slice onion into strips, start by cutting off both ends of the onion and removing the outer skin. Slice onion in half from stem to root and lay halves flat side down on cutting board. Make ½ inch parallel cuts across the onion and separate into strips.

Arroz con Pollo

Chicken with Rice

Arroz con pollo is a classic Latin dish with many variations. Consuelo's salsa verde (green sauce) version of chicken and rice is an easy, one pot, delicious meal.

INGREDIENTS

4 cloves garlic

1 large onion, halved

1 teaspoon paprika

4 cups fresh spinach (about 6 ounces)

½ cup fresh cilantro

2 teaspoons salt, plus extra for sprinkling

Black pepper to taste

2 ½ cups water, divided (see Tips for Success)

1 tablespoon vegetable oil

6 assorted pieces of chicken

2 cups long grain rice

½ cup frozen carrots

½ cup frozen corn

½ cup frozen peas

SERVES: 4-6

Combine garlic, onion, paprika, spinach, cilantro, 2 tsp. salt, pepper, and ½ cup water in blender. Blend on high until smooth. Measure the amount and set aside.

Sprinkle chicken pieces with a little salt. Heat 1 Tbsp. oil in a large skillet or Dutch oven over medium-high heat and sear chicken, 3 pieces at a time, until skin is brown and crispy; be careful of the splattering oil! Remove and set aside. Drain and discard all but 1 tablespoon of grease.

Return pan to medium-high heat, and add contents of blender. Cook 2-3 minutes, scraping brown bits to deglaze pan and incorporate flavors. Add rice and stir well to coat. Add frozen vegetables and 2 cups water (see Tips for Success), stir. Place chicken pieces on top and pour in any accumulated juices. Bring to boil, reduce heat, and cover. Maintain simmer for about 30 minutes, or until water is absorbed, rice is fluffy, and chicken is no longer pink.

Serve immediately on warm plates.

TIPS FOR SUCCESS

• To get the right amount of water, first check your rice instructions to find out the ratio (I typically use long grain white rice with a 2:1 ratio). Measure the contents of liquid in the blender (it should be around 2 cups), and subtract this amount from the total amount of water needed for the rice. For example: when preparing rice with a 2:1 ratio, I would typically use 4 cups of water to 2 cups of rice; but in this recipe, I subtract the 2 cups of liquid in the blender from the total and only add 1¾-2 cups of water to pan. I also take into account that the chicken will be releasing juices.

Pollo con Hongos

Chicken with Mushrooms

This weeknight meal is simple, yet packed with juicy flavor. It goes well over rice to soak up the sauce. Thighs are best known for moistness and flavor, but you can substitute your favorite cut of chicken. If you are a mushroom lover, feel free to double the amount.

INGREDIENTS

10-12 skinless chicken thighs

½ teaspoon salt

5 tablespoons soy sauce

1 tablespoon ginger, grated

2 tablespoons vegetable oil, divided

6 thin slices of ginger

1 pound fresh mushrooms, halved

1-2 tablespoons water

2 tablespoons potato or corn starch whisked into ¼ cup cold water

Hot rice

4 green onions, sliced (optional)

SERVES: 4-6

Sprinkle chicken with salt and place in large dish or re-sealable plastic bag. Stir together soy sauce and grated ginger, pour over chicken, cover, and refrigerate at least 30 minutes, or up to 4 hours.

Heat wok or heavy-duty pan over high heat. Add 1 Tbsp. oil and heat just until smoking. Add sliced ginger and fry 30 seconds. Add another Tbsp. oil and mushrooms and stir-fry 2-3 minutes, stirring or tossing mushrooms constantly.

Reduce heat to medium-high. Add chicken pieces and 1-2 Tbsp. water, stir, cover, and bring to a boil. Reduce heat to medium to maintain a steady simmer and cook 20-30 minutes or until no longer pink.

Increase heat to high, make a well in the center of the wok and pour in starch mixture. Stir and cook 1-2 minutes until thickened and all food is well coated in sauce.

Serve immediately over hot rice on warm plates and sprinkle with green onions (if using).

Peru is a surfer's paradise. Chicama has the world's longest left-handed wave at 4 km long, and Mancora (close by) has the world's largest left-handed point-break.

Arroz Chaufa

Fried Rice

Even the pickiest of eaters can't resist the enthralling Asian flavors of fried rice. This meal is every cook's dream: easy, fast, and always a hit! We love to pack this in Chinese to-go boxes and take it to the beach for a picnic.

INGREDIENTS

2 pounds boneless,
skinless chicken breasts,
cut into ½ inch cubes

2-3 teaspoons ginger, grated

Black pepper, to taste

6 tablespoons soy sauce, divided

8 eggs

¼ teaspoon salt

2 tablespoons butter, divided

2-3 tablespoons vegetable oil

6 cups cooked rice, cold (best made a day ahead with a little extra oil and refrigerated)

5 green onions, thinly sliced

SERVES: 4-6

Stir together chicken, ginger, black pepper, and 4 Tbsp. soy sauce in a medium size bowl. Cover, refrigerate, and let marinate at least 30 minutes or up to 4 hours.

Meanwhile, prepare omelets by beating the eggs and salt in a large bowl until frothy. Heat 1 Tbsp. of butter in an omelet pan over medium-high heat just until it starts to lightly brown. Pour in ½ of the eggs and allow to cook until beginning to set. Tilt the pan and lift the edges to allow un-cooked eggs to run underneath. When the omelet is golden brown on the bottom, quickly flip. Continue cooking until light and fluffy. Remove from pan, and repeat process. Dice into bite size pieces and set aside.

Place large wok over high heat and add 1 Tbsp. oil just until smoking. Using a slotted spoon, add ½ of the chicken, spread across wok, and let sear 1 minute. Turn and sear other side. Stir, cover, and cook 2-3 minutes more or until no longer pink. Remove and keep warm. Repeat with remaining chicken, reserving excess marinade, and leaving second batch in wok.

Add 1 Tbsp. oil to wok if needed, and add cooked chicken and rice. Stir well to mix. Add 1-2 Tbsp. soy sauce, omelet, green onions, and reserved marinade, and stir well. Cover and cook 2-3 minutes or until very hot.

Serve immediately on warm plates.

The Inca citadel of Machu Picchu was lost to the Amazon jungle for hundreds of years, until it was re-discovered by Hiram Bingham, the American explorer.

Paticay

White Cut Chicken – Bak Chit Gai

There is a funny story behind the name of this recipe. While in Peru, working on finalizing recipes, I asked my husband and Consuelo how to spell the name of this dish. They looked at each other in a puzzled way and said, "I don't really know, it's a Chinese word," and they made up the spelling. Upon returning home and doing my research, I could not find any Chinese recipe called "Paticay." However, I did find an identical recipe called "Bak Chit Gai." At first we were confused, and then we realized, years ago when Pancho said the words, "Bak Chit Gai," in Spanish, with his heavy Chinese accent, his family thought he was saying, "Paticay." So to this day, we still call it that and smile!

INGREDIENTS

1 whole chicken

2 teaspoons salt, divided

¼ cup vegetable oil

2 teaspoons ginger, grated

Black pepper, to taste

1 pinch of hot red pepper flakes

2 green onions, thinly sliced

Soy sauce for dipping

SERVES: 4-6

Rinse and dry chicken. Lightly rub 1 tsp. salt over skin and in cavity. Place in large pot with enough water to cover. Add 1 tsp. salt to water.

Place pot over high heat and bring to a gentle boil. Cover, reduce heat, and gently simmer 30 minutes or until no longer pink. Remove and let drain. Place on cutting board.

While the chicken simmers, prepare sauce. Pour oil into a small saucepan over medium heat. Add grated ginger, pinch of salt, black pepper, and hot pepper flakes. Carefully warm over medium-low heat.

With a large, heavy-duty cleaver, chop chicken into pieces a little larger than bite size. Don't be afraid to use a strong forceful chop to cut through the bones. Or you may prefer to cut the meat away from the bones before serving. Place meat on a pre-warmed platter, sprinkle with green onions, and pour hot oil over top.

Serve with soy sauce and chopsticks.

Peru's Huascarán National Park has more has 27 snow-capped peaks 6,000 meters (19,685 feet) above sea level, of which El Huascarán (6,768 meters / 22,204 feet) is the highest.

Aji de Gallina

Chicken Chile

"Don't judge a book by its cover," applies well to one of our personal favorites, as well as one of Peru's favorites, Aji de Gallina! Imagine your taste buds coming alive as they savor tender chicken bathed in a nutty cream sauce, followed by a hint of heat. Just writing this makes my mouth water! I find it even more delicious the next day, or as a filling in empanadas (page 69).

INGREDIENTS

1 whole chicken (3 ½-4 pounds), skin and excess fat removed, and cut into parts

2½ teaspoons salt, divided

1 cup pecans, peanuts, or walnuts soaked in fresh water 1 hour or more and drained (see Tips for Success)

4 slices white bread, crust removed and cubed

1 large yellow onion

2 tablespoons vegetable oil

2-4 tablespoons aji amarillo paste, depending on hot you like it

3 cloves garlic, pressed

¼ teaspoon nutmeg

1 (12 ounce) can evaporated milk

½ cup Parmesan cheese, grated

Hot rice

3 hard boiled eggs, halved

Aceitunas (Peruvian olives)

SERVES: 4-6

Place chicken and 1 tsp. salt in a large pot with just enough water to cover. Bring to a gentle boil over high heat, cover, reduce heat, and simmer 20 minutes or until no longer pink.

Remove chicken and let cool. Reserve water. Shred or cube chicken and set aside. This step can be done a day ahead and refrigerated (see Tips for Success).

Blend nuts, bread, and ¾-1 cup reserved chicken water on high until smooth. Remove and set aside. Rinse blender.

Blend onion and ¼-½ cup reserved water until pureed. Remove and set aside.

Heat 2 Tbsp. of the oil in a large pot over medium heat until shimmering. Add pureed onion and cook 10 minutes, stirring as necessary to keep from sticking.

Add 1 tsp. salt, aji, garlic, nutmeg, and ⅔ cup reserved water, stir and cook another 10 minutes.

Add pecan puree and stir and cook about 8-10 minutes. Stir in evaporated milk, cheese, and chicken. Cook another 5 minutes, taste and adjust seasonings if necessary

Serve over hot rice on warm plate, garnished with eggs and olives.

TIPS FOR SUCCESS

• If you choose to cook your chicken a day ahead, douse the shredded chicken with some of the reserved broth and seal tightly to maintain moistness.

• If you prefer all white meat, use 4 or 5 split breasts instead of 1 whole chicken.

• For an easy shortcut, try using a rotisserie chicken from your favorite store or deli and canned broth. Discard skin, remove meat from bones and shred. Follow with recipe beginning at step 3.

• "Aji de Gallina a la Americana," translation: slow-cooker version! Take 1 teaspoon salt, soaked pecans, bread, oil, onion (quartered), aji paste, garlic, and nutmeg, and blend with 2 cups chicken broth until smooth and creamy. Pour ½ into slow-cooker, lay 4 chicken breasts over sauce, and pour remaining sauce over chicken. Cook on medium 4 hours or until chicken is very tender and easily pulls apart. Shred chicken, return to slow-cooker, and stir in evaporated milk and Parmesan cheese. Cook another ½ hour on low. Times may vary according to individual slow-cookers.

• When using walnuts, the skin can add a bitter taste. They are best when soaked for several hours and then peeled. My husband remembers his mother spending time doing this process, and the results are worth it. I prefer to use pecans and the skin does not need to be removed.

TIPS FOR SUCCESS

• Keep the leafy part of the nappa to be used in Saltado de Nappa (page 110).

• Sugar snap peas make a nice replacement for snow peas.

Saltado de Pollo con Vegetales

Chicken Stir-fry with Vegetables

This is another wonderful stir-fry packed full of nutrition, textures, and flavors. It can be served over rice, or even better, over Chinese noodles, as pictured here.

INGREDIENTS

2 pounds boneless chicken breast, cut into small bite size pieces

7 tablespoons soy sauce, divided

2 teaspoons ginger, grated

Pinch of granulated sugar

Black pepper, to taste

1 pound Chinese noodles or hot rice

5 tablespoons vegetable oil, divided

6 thin slices of ginger

2 cups nappa (1 pound head), stalk only, diced

½ cup celery, diced

1 cup snow peas (about ¼ pound), halved on bias

1 small bell pepper, diced or sliced into thin strips

5 green onions, sliced into 1 inch pieces on bias

2 tablespoons potato or corn starch whisked into ¼ cup cold water

½ cup roasted nuts, roughly chopped

SERVES: 4-6

In a large bowl, stir together chicken, 4 Tbsp. soy sauce, grated ginger, sugar, and black pepper. Cover and refrigerate at least 30 minutes or up to 4 hours.

Cook Chinese noodles, if using, according to package. Drain well and toss with 2 tbsp. soy sauce and 2 tbsp. oil. Cover and set aside.

In a large wok or heavy-duty pan, heat 1 Tbsp. oil over high heat just until smoking. Add sliced ginger and fry 30 seconds. Add nappa and stir-fry until just beginning to char, about 1 minute. Add remaining vegetables, stir-fry for 1 minute and add 1 Tbsp. soy sauce. Cover quickly and steam 1 minute more until vegetables are tender-crisp (more on the crisp side), remove and cover to keep warm.

Return wok to high heat and add 1 Tbsp. oil until smoking. Using slotted spoon, add ½ of the chicken, spread across wok in single layer, and sear 1 minute. Turn and sear another minute. Stir, cover, and cook 3-4 minutes or just until no longer pink. Remove and add to vegetables. Repeat process with remaining chicken, reserving excess marinade, and leaving second batch in wok.

Return all meat, vegetables, and reserved marinade to wok over medium-high heat. Stir and make a well in the center. Pour starch mixture into the well, stir, and cook 1-2 minutes to thicken sauce.

Serve immediately on warm plates over noodles or rice, and garnish with nuts.

Saltado de Nappa

Chicken Stir-fry with Nappa

Like most stir-fry dishes, this one is quick, simple, and oh so delicious—not to mention healthy! The roasted nuts add the perfect crunch and the nappa stalk can be used for Saltado de Pollo con Vegetales (page 109).

INGREDIENTS

2½ pounds boneless chicken breast, cut into small bite size pieces

5 tablespoons soy sauce

Black pepper, to taste

2 teaspoons ginger, grated

3 tablespoons vegetable oil, divided

6 thin slices of ginger

2 pound head of nappa, leafy part only, sliced

2 tablespoons potato or corn starch whisked into ¼ cup cold water

Hot rice

½ cup roasted nuts, roughly chopped

SERVES: 4-6

In a large bowl, stir together chicken, soy sauce, black pepper, and grated ginger. Cover and refrigerate at least 30 minutes or up to 4 hours.

In a large wok or heavy-duty pan, heat 1 Tbsp. oil over high heat just until smoking. Add ginger slices and fry 30 seconds. Add nappa leaves and stir-fry 1 minute, until leaves are slightly charred and beginning to wilt. Remove from wok and cover to keep warm.

Return wok to high heat, add 1 Tbsp. oil and using a slotted spoon, add ½ of the chicken. Spread in single layer across wok and sear 1 minute. Turn and sear another minute. Stir, cover, and cook 1-2 minutes more until no longer pink. Remove and add to nappa. Repeat process with remaining chicken, reserving excess marinade and leaving second batch in wok.

Return chicken, nappa, and reserved marinade to wok over medium-high heat. Stir and make a well in the center. Pour in the starch mixture and cook 1-2 minutes until thick and coated.

Serve immediately with hot rice on warm plates and garnish with nuts.

Two-thirds of Peru is covered in prime Amazon Rain Forest.

Pollo Saltado

Chicken Stir-fry

This chicken is super easy and super delicious. It is made with bone-in chicken which adds so much more flavor than boneless. To make it easy, I recommend having the butcher pre-cut your chicken for you. It's fun to eat with chop sticks!

INGREDIENTS

1 large whole chicken, cut into bite size pieces

5 tablespoons soy sauce

2 tablespoons vegetable oil

Pinch of sugar

3 thin slices ginger

2 tablespoons potato or corn starch

2 tablespoons Heinz ketchup

¼ cup cold water

Hot rice

SERVES: 4-6

In a large bowl or resealable plastic bag, combine chicken and soy sauce and marinate in refrigerator for 30 minutes or up to 4 hours.

Heat oil in wok or heavy-duty pan over high heat, just until smoking and sprinkle with a pinch of sugar. Add ginger slices and fry for 30 seconds. Using a slotted spoon, add chicken pieces, spread across wok, and sear 1-2 minutes. Stir and sear another 1-2 minutes until chicken is golden and begins to release juices. Stir in any excess marinade.

Cover, reduce heat to medium, and cook until no longer pink, about 15-20 minutes.

Mix together starch, ketchup, and cold water until smooth. Make a well in center of chicken, and pour in mixture. Cook and stir 1-2 minutes more until thickened and chicken is well coated.

Serve immediately with rice on warm plates.

The Amazon river, which starts in Peru, is the largest river in the world by volume.

Machu Picchu, Peru

Saltado de Pollo con Piña

Chicken Stir-fry with Pineapple

This succulent Chinese stir-fry is a blend of sweet and savory to perfection. The tender crisp green beans, contrasting with the chunks of fresh pineapple make it a hit for all ages.

INGREDIENTS

2 pounds boneless chicken breast, cut into small bite size pieces

5 tablespoons soy sauce

2 teaspoons ginger, grated

Black pepper, to taste

3 tablespoons vegetable oil, divided

3 cups fresh green beans (about ¾ pound), sliced in half on bias

2 tablespoons cold water

10 green onions, light portion only, sliced on bias into 1 inch pieces

1 fresh pineapple, about 4 cups, cubed into bite size chunks

1 (8 ounce) jar whole mushrooms, undrained

2 tablespoons potato or corn starch whisked into ¼ cup cold water

Hot rice

SERVES: 4-6

In a large bowl stir together chicken, soy sauce, ginger, and black pepper. Cover and refrigerate at least 30 minutes or up to 4 hours.

In a large wok or heavy-duty pan, heat 1 Tbsp. oil over high heat just until smoking. Add green beans and stir-fry 1 minute; they should begin to lightly char. Add 2 Tbsp. water, cover quickly, reduce heat to medium-high, and steam 2½ minutes until tender crisp, stirring if needed. Remove beans, cover, and keep warm.

Return wok to high heat and add another Tbsp. oil until smoking. Using a slotted spoon, add ½ of the chicken and spread in a single layer across the wok. Let sear 1 minute, turn and sear another minute. Stir and cook 2-3 minutes more until no longer pink. Remove from wok and add to green beans. Repeat with remaining chicken, reserving excess marinade, and then remove second batch of chicken from wok.

Add green onions to wok and stir-fry 1 minute. Return green beans and chicken to wok. Stir in pineapple with any accumulated juice, reserved marinade, and mushrooms with liquid. Cover and bring to boil.

Make a well in center of the wok and stir in the starch mixture. Cook 1-2 minutes until thickened and gently stir until all food is nicely coated with sauce.

Serve immediately with rice on warm plates.

Lima is the largest province in Peru, with some eight million residents.

Lomo Saltado

Peruvian Style Beef Stir-fry

Consuelo put her Asian spin on this very traditional Peruvian dish by incorporating ginger and soy sauce. This recipe is easy to prepare, requires no special ingredients, and is beautifully impressive for guests. When I make this, friends and family always refer to it as, "The one with the French fries on top!"

INGREDIENTS

1½ pounds top round, sirloin, or flank steak, thinly sliced and cut to 1½ inch strips against grain

4-5 tablespoons soy sauce

2 cloves garlic, pressed

Black pepper, to taste

2 teaspoons ginger, grated

6 cups canola or corn oil

2½ pounds Yukon gold or Idaho potatoes, sliced into ¼ inch strips

Salt to taste

1 tablespoon Heinz ketchup

2 tablespoons potato or corn starch

2 tablespoons cold water, divided

3 tablespoons vegetable oil, divided

6 thin slices of ginger

1 large sweet or red onion, cut into ½ inch strips (see Tips for Success)

2 stalks celery, cut into 1 inch thinly sliced strips

½ teaspoon salt

2 tomatoes, seeded and diced

Hot rice

SERVES: 4-6

In a medium size bowl, stir together beef, soy sauce, garlic, black pepper, and grated ginger. Cover and refrigerate at least 30 minutes or up to 4 hours.

While meat is marinating, prepare French fries by filling a large pot with 6 cups canola/corn oil and potatoes. Turn heat to high, bring to boil, and continue boiling on high, uncovered for 15 minutes without stirring. After 15 minutes, use tongs to gently stir and release potatoes from bottom of pot. Continue to fry until golden, about 10-15 minutes more. Use spider strainer to remove fries from hot oil and place in paper towel lined bowl, sprinkle with salt and set aside.

While potatoes are cooking, mix Heinz ketchup with potato starch and 1 Tbsp. cold water and set aside.

Begin this step when potatoes are at the 15 minute mark. In a wok or heavy bottom pan, heat 1 Tbsp. vegetable oil over high heat just until smoking. Add sliced ginger and fry 30 seconds.

Add onion, celery, and salt, and stir-fry 2 minutes. Add 1 Tbsp. water, cover immediately to steam and cook 1 minute more. Vegetables should be tender-crisp. Remove from pan and cover to keep warm.

Add another Tbsp. vegetable oil to wok over high heat until smoking. Using slotted spoon, add ½ of the beef mixture and sear 1 minute, turn and sear other side. Stir, cover, and cook 1-2 minutes until barely pink. Remove, add to vegetables, and keep warm. Repeat process with remaining beef, reserving excess marinade.

Return beef, vegetables, and reserved marinade to wok and stir in tomatoes. Reduce heat to medium-high, cover and cook 1 minute. Push food to side to make well in center, stir in ketchup mixture and stir and cook to thicken. If timed properly, French fries and Lomo will be done at the same time.

Serve immediately on warm plates with hot rice, topped with French fries.

TIPS FOR SUCCESS

• This dish is a perfect one to start with when you are new to Peruvian cooking. It is a standard on Peruvian menus and is easy for a beginner. Be sure to have all your ingredients prepped ahead of time, and cooking will be a breeze.

• If you really do not have the time or desire to make your own French fries, frozen ones will work too, but these fries are so easy to make and guests are always in awe to have homemade French fries!

• If you are preparing fries for a large crowd and plan on making a double batch, you will need to make adjustments, and factor in extra time. A larger amount of water will be released from the potatoes, and they can quickly turn into a pile of mush. You can either divide them into two single batches if you have the extra burner space, or double the recipe in 1 large pot. If you choose to double the recipe, wait close to 25 minutes at a full boil before attempting to gently stir and release fries from bottom of the pot. Continue frying another 15-20 minutes, stirring gently only once or twice more.

• To slice onion into strips, start by cutting off both ends of the onion and removing the outer skin. Slice onion in half from stem to root and lay halves flat side down on cutting board. Make ½ inch parallel cuts across the onion and separate into strips.

Saltado de Vainitas con Papas Fritas

Beef Stir-fry with Green Beans and Fried Potatoes

Another great marriage of East and West cuisine! I love the crunchy texture of the crisp green beans and the bite of the ginger; don't forget, it wouldn't be Peruvian without the addition of fried potatoes.

INGREDIENTS

1½ pounds top round, sirloin, or flank steak, thinly sliced and cut into 1½ inch strips against the grain

4 tablespoons soy sauce

Black pepper, to taste

1 tablespoon ginger, grated

½ teaspoon salt

4 cups fresh green beans (about 1 pound), sliced on bias into 1 inch pieces

2½ pounds Yukon gold or Idaho potatoes, cut into ½ inch cubes

6 cups canola or corn oil

2 tablespoons vegetable oil, divided

6 thin slices of ginger

Hot rice

SERVES: 4-6

In a large bowl, stir together beef, soy sauce, black pepper, and grated ginger. Cover, refrigerate, and marinate at least 30 minutes or up to 4 hours.

In a medium sauce pan, bring 3 cups water to boil, add salt and green beans. Boil about 4 minutes, drain and immediately immerse green beans in a bowl of ice water. Cool 2-3 minutes, drain well, and set aside.

While meat is marinating, prepare potatoes by filling a large pot with potato cubes and 6 cups canola/corn oil and place over high heat. Bring to boil and continue boiling uncovered on high for at least 15 minutes without touching. At this point, stir to release any potatoes from bottom. Continue frying for another 10-15 minutes until golden. Remove from hot oil with spider strainer and place in paper towel lined bowl. Sprinkle lightly with salt and set aside.

When potatoes are at 15 minute mark, place wok or heavy-duty pan over high heat and add 1 Tbsp. vegetable oil just until smoking. Add slices of ginger and fry 30 seconds. Using slotted spoon, add ½ of the meat to wok and spread across in single layer. Sear 1 minute, turn, and sear another minute. Stir, cover, and cook 3-4 minutes until barely pink. Remove and keep warm. Repeat process with remaining beef, reserving excess marinade, and leaving second batch in wok.

Return beef to wok over medium-high heat and stir in green beans and reserved marinade. Cover and cook 1-2 minutes. Add potatoes, stir gently to mix, cover, and cook 1-2 minutes more until steaming hot. If timed properly, stir-fry and potatoes will be ready at the same time.

Serve immediately with hot rice on warm plates.

Saltado de Coliflor

Beef Stir-fry with Cauliflower

What really makes this stir-fry come alive is the cilantro; if you have already decided you do not like cilantro, give it another chance and I guarantee you will be pleasantly surprised! You can top off this dish with papas fritas (fried potato cubes) for a Peruvian-Chinese fusion.

INGREDIENTS

1½ pounds top round, sirloin, or flank steak, thinly sliced and cut into 1½ inch strips against the grain

3 tablespoons black bean sauce with garlic

Black pepper, to taste

1 tablespoon ginger, grated

2-3 tablespoons soy sauce

3 tablespoons vegetable oil, divided

1 head of cauliflower, cut into small florets

Salt, to taste

¼ cup water

6 thin slices of ginger

2 tablespoons potato or corn starch whisked into ¼ cup cold water

¾ cup cilantro, minced

Hot rice

2½ pounds Yukon gold or Idaho potatoes, cubed and fried until golden and crispy (optional, see Tips for Success)

SERVES: 4-6

In a medium size bowl, stir together beef, black bean sauce, black pepper, grated ginger, and soy sauce. Cover, refrigerate, and let marinate at least 30 minutes or up to 4 hours.

Heat 1 Tbsp. oil over high heat in a wok or heavy-duty pan, just until smoking. Add cauliflower and stir-fry about 2 minutes until it begins to slightly char. Add a pinch of salt and ¼ cup of water. Cover quickly and steam until al dente, about 3 minutes. Remove from wok, cover, and keep warm.

Return wok to high heat and add another Tbsp. oil until smoking. Add sliced ginger and fry for 30 seconds. Using slotted spoon, add ½ of the beef mixture, spread across wok in single layer, and let sear 1 minute. Turn and sear other side 1 minute. Stir and cook about 2-3 minutes until barely pink. Remove and add to cauliflower. Heat last Tbsp. of oil and repeat with remaining beef, reserving excess marinade, and leave second batch of meat in wok.

Return beef and cauliflower to wok, along with any juices and reserved marinade. Push food to the side of the wok to create a well in the center, pour in the starch mixture

Cotahuasi Canyon in the Arequipa region is considered one of the world's deepest canyons – twice as deep as the Grand Canyon, USA.

and gently stir to cook and thicken. Stir in cilantro, cover, and cook 1 more minute.

Serve immediately with rice on warm plates, topped with fried potatoes (if using).

Saltado de Carne con Foo Gwa

Beef Stir-fry with Bitter Melon

"Eat Bitter" is a Chinese maxim to teach children about the hardships of life. Saltado de Carne con Foo Gwa exemplifies this proverb, literally! But don't let the word "bitter" turn you away; it's an acquired taste you will soon learn to love. Foo gwa is a Chinese bitter melon (also called bitter cucumber), and has long been reputable in Eastern medicine for a multitude of health benefits. Taking note of this, Western medicine is beginning to recognize its beneficial properties too. My advice? Eat bitter, it's good for you.

INGREDIENTS

2 pounds top round, sirloin, or flank steak, thinly sliced and cut into 1½ inch strips against the grain

1 tablespoon black bean sauce with garlic

4 tablespoons soy sauce

A pinch of sugar

Black pepper to taste

1 teaspoon salt

1 bitter cucumber (about ½ pound)

2 tablespoons potato or corn starch mixed into ¼ cup cold water

Hot rice

SERVES: 4-6

TIPS FOR SUCCESS
• This is equally delicious prepared with pork tenderloin rather than beef.

In a medium size bowl, stir together beef, black bean sauce, soy sauce, sugar, and black pepper. Cover, refrigerate, and let marinate at least 30 minutes or up to 4 hours.

While meat is marinating, prepare cucumber. Remove ends (do not peel), slice in half lengthwise, scrape, and remove seeds and white pith with a spoon. Cut on bias into small slices about ¼ inch wide.

Bring a medium size saucepan full of water to a boil over high heat. Add salt and cucumber and boil 3 minutes. Drain well and set aside. This step helps to reduce the bitterness.

In a large wok or heavy-duty pan, heat 1 Tbsp. oil over high heat just until smoking. Using a slotted spoon, add ½ the beef mixture, and spread in single layer across wok. Let sear about 1 minute, turn, and sear another minute. Stir and let cook 2-3 minutes or until barely pink. Remove, cover, and keep warm. Repeat process with remaining beef, reserving excess marinade, and leaving second batch in wok.

Return beef to wok, along with accumulated juices and reserved marinade. Add cucumber and cook 1 minute. Make well in center and pour in starch mixture. Stir gently and cook 1-2 minutes to thicken sauce.

Serve immediately with hot rice on warm plates.

TIPS FOR SUCCESS

• For a sweet addition, add ½ cup raisins when adding vegetables to stew.

• Be sure to use stew beef, and do not to rush the cooking time. If the meat is not cooked long enough, it will be tough. You want it to be so tender that you can cut it with your fork; I guarantee it will be worth the wait!

Estofado de Carne

Beef Stew

Estofado simply translates to stew; it seems every culture has this staple family meal, each with its own unique flavors. What makes the Peruvian version so delicious is the incorporation of the aji panca mixed with the depth of the red wine. If you don't have aji available, you can substitute tomato paste, but for me, then it becomes just any stew.

INGREDIENTS

2 tablespoons vegetable oil

1 medium onion, finely chopped

4 cloves garlic, pressed

1 large tomato, peeled, seeded, and diced

1 teaspoon cumin

1-2 tablespoons aji panca paste, depending on how hot you like it

1½ teaspoons salt

Black pepper, to taste

3 pounds beef chuck roast, cut into 1½-2 inch cubes

1 bay leaf

Splash of red wine or red wine vinegar

2 carrots, thinly sliced

2 potatoes, diced small (optional)

1 cup frozen peas

2 tablespoons potato or corn starch whisked into ¼ cup cold water

Hot rice

SERVES: 4-6

In a large pot or Dutch oven, heat oil over medium-high heat. Add onion and cook for 3-4 minutes. Stir and adjust heat to keep from burning. Add garlic, tomatoes, cumin, aji panca, salt, and pepper. Cook 2-3 minutes, adding a tablespoon of water if necessary to keep from sticking.

Add beef, bay leaf, and wine/vinegar. Stir to coat. Cover and reduce heat to simmer 1½-2 hours. Stir in carrots and potatoes, (if using) and continue to simmer for 30 minutes, or until meat and vegetables are tender. Stir in peas and cook and additional 5 minutes.

Push food to side to make a well in center, increase heat and stir in starch mixture. Cook and stir 1-2 minutes until thickened and food is evenly coated in sauce. Remove bay leaf.

Serve over hot rice on warm plates.

TIPS FOR SUCCESS

• This is another successful recipe that I have adapted to a slow-cooker version, using either cubed stew beef or a 2½ lb. pot roast. If you will be gone all day and will not be home until dinner, use this method: slice carrots and potatoes a little thicker than directed, and start with step 1 by sautéing the onions and spices. Next, put remaining ingredients in crock pot, except starch mixture and rice. Pour onion mixture overtop of meat. Cook on high 4-6 hours, or low 6-8 hours, or until meat it very tender and almost falls apart. Stir in starch mixture during the last 10 minutes of cooking. If you are home while this is in the slow-cooker, follow this method: do not add carrots, potatoes (if using), or peas with the beef. Wait until halfway through cooking before adding carrots and potatoes, and stir in peas and starch mixture in the last 10 minutes of cooking. Times vary by individual slow-cookers.

Estofado de Lengua

Beef Tongue Stew

This will be the most tender meat you will ever eat and is a rare delicacy. It truly melts in your mouth and is easily cut with a fork. This is my husband's favorite Father's Day dinner!

INGREDIENTS

1 fresh beef tongue, 2-3 pounds

2 tablespoons vegetable oil

1 medium onion finely chopped

3 cloves garlic, pressed

1-2 tablespoons aji panca paste, depending on hot you like it

½ teaspoon dried oregano

1½ teaspoons salt

Black pepper, to taste

2-3 carrots, thinly sliced

1 cup frozen peas

2 tablespoons potato or corn starch whisked into ¼ cup cold water

Hot rice

¼ cup fresh parsley, chopped

SERVES: 4-6

Take the fresh tongue and rinse it very well. Place it in a large stock pot and cover with cold water. Bring to a gentle boil over high heat, cover, and reduce heat to maintain a simmer.

Simmer for 2 hours or more until tender and pierces easily with fork. Remove meat and reserve water. Using a sharp knife, remove and discard outer coating; it should peel right off. Slice meat to about 1/3-½ inch thick. Set aside.

Heat oil in a large pot over medium-high heat and cook onion 3-4 minutes. Add garlic, aji panca, oregano, salt, and black pepper, cook 1-2 minutes more. Add carrots and 2 cups of reserved beef water and bring to boil. Cover, reduce heat, and simmer 10 minutes.

Add peas and sliced meat to pot. Cook 8-10 minutes more or until carrots are tender and pierce easily with a fork. Stir in starch mixture to thicken.

Serve over hot rice on warm plates and sprinkle with parsley.

TIPS FOR SUCCESS

• It is important to simmer the tongue until very tender; otherwise, it may be tough. Do not rush this step.

• This dish is one that is even better the next day as the beef has time to marinate in the flavors of the sauce.

• The fresh tongue may also be simmered in a slow-cooker bathed in water on low for 6-8 hours until fork tender and then peeled and sliced. Proceed with step 3 of recipe to complete, or refrigerate for later use.

Estofado de Nabo

Beef and Radish Stew

This is a traditional Cantonese beef stew with a unique taste derived from the radish and black bean paste. It is quite different from the two previous estofado recipes featured in this collection. While visiting Peru for Consuleo's 90th birthday, we sat around discussing our favorite foods. My brother-in-law, who is very picky, said one of his favorites was Estofado de Nabo. I had not heard of this nor ever tasted it. Immediately, I turned to Consuelo to pick her brain about the recipe, and I couldn't help but wonder, how many other recipes has she forgotten to share with me?

INGREDIENTS

3 pounds beef chuck roast, cut into 1½ inch cubes

1 tablespoon vegetable oil

5 slices of ginger

1-2 teaspoons ginger, grated

2 tablespoons black bean paste with garlic

2 cups water

1 teaspoon salt

1 medium nabo (Daikon radish, about 2 pounds) cut into ½ inch cubes

2 tablespoons potato or corn starch whisked into ¼ cup cold water

5 green onions, thinly sliced

Soy sauce to taste

Hot rice

SERVES: 4-6

Place meat in a medium sized saucepan, add enough water to cover, and place over high heat. Bring to a gentle boil and adjust heat to maintain a steady simmer for 5 minutes. Skim and discard brown foam covering top of water. Remove from heat, drain, and rinse meat. Set aside.

Heat 1 Tbsp. oil in a large Dutch oven over medium high heat until shimmering. Fry ginger slices 1 minute or until golden. Stir in grated ginger and black bean paste and continue to cook another 3-4 minutes, lowering heat if necessary. Add beef and stir to coat.

Add 2 cups fresh water and 1 tsp. salt. Bring to boil, reduce heat, cover and simmer 1 hour.

Add radish cubes and continue to simmer until radish looks translucent, about 45-60 minutes. Stir in starch mixture and cook another minute or two until thick.

Stir in green onions and 2 Tbsp. soy sauce.

Serve on warm plate over hot rice with additional soy sauce.

The finest cottons in the world, Pima and Tanguis, are Peruvian.

TIPS FOR SUCCESS

• Do not skip step 1, blanching the meat. This process removes unwanted proteins that cause the familiar brown foam when simmering beef. It produces a beautifully clear broth in the finished product.

• If your black bean paste is without garlic, add 3 pressed cloves of garlic when you add the beef in step 2.

• Slow-cooker variation: start with step 1, and place blanched meat in slow-cooker with grated ginger, black bean paste, salt, nabo, and 2 cups of water. In a small sauté pan, fry ginger slices in hot oil and stir into slow-cooker with other ingredients. Cook on high 4-6 hours, or low 6-8 hours, or until meat and nabo are tender. Stir in starch mixture until thickened, and stir in green onions and soy sauce. Serve as directed. Times may vary according to individual slow-cookers.

Tallarines Criollos

Coastal Style Noodles

If you love pasta, this is a dish for you! A combination of beef stir-fry and fettuccine noodles at their best! The hint of vinegar adds a mouth-watering touch. Again we have a union of Peruvian and Asian flavors. Remember, noodles most likely originated in China, not Italy, contrary to popular belief.

INGREDIENTS

1½ pounds top round, sirloin, or flank steak, thinly sliced and cut into 1½ inch strips against the grain

½ teaspoon cumin

1 tablespoon aji panca paste

5 tablespoons soy sauce, divided

2 teaspoons red wine vinegar

5-6 tablespoons vegetable oil, divided

Black pepper, to taste

2 cloves garlic, minced

2 teaspoons ginger, grated

1 pound fettuccine noodles

1 sweet or red onion, cut into ½ inch slices (see Tips for Success)

1 teaspoon paprika

6 thin slices of ginger

2 tomatoes, seeded and diced

SERVES: 4-6

In a large bowl, stir together beef, cumin, aji panca, 3 Tbsp. soy sauce, vinegar, 2 tsp.oil, black pepper, garlic, and grated ginger. Cover, refrigerate, and let marinate at least 30 minutes or up to 4 hours.

Cook pasta as directed and drain well. Stir in 2 Tbsp. oil and 2 Tbsp. soy sauce. Cover and set aside.

Place wok or heavy-duty pan over high heat and add 1 Tbsp. oil just until smoking. Add onions and stir-fry 2-3 minutes. Sprinkle with paprika and stir-fry 1 minute more. Remove from wok, cover, and keep warm.

Return wok to high heat and add another Tbsp. oil until smoking. Add sliced ginger and fry 30 seconds. Using slotted spoon, add ½ of the beef, spread across wok in a single layer, and sear 1 minute. Turn and sear another minute. Stir and cook 2-3 minutes more until barely pink. Remove from wok and add to onions. Repeat process with remaining beef, reserving excess marinade, and leaving second batch in wok.

Return beef and onions to wok and stir in tomatoes and reserved marinade. Reduce heat to medium, cover, and cook 1 minute until steaming hot.

Serve immediately over pasta on warm plates.

Carne al Vapor

Steamed Beef

Carne al vapor is made with chung choy, which has a somewhat sweet and chewy, salty flavor. Together with tender steamed beef, the dish has unique textures that are hard to describe, yet are oh so good. Pancho prepared this Cantonese dish many years ago for his family; I never had the pleasure of knowing my father-in-law, but his presence is felt at the table when we enjoy his recipes.

INGREDIENTS

2 pounds top round, thinly sliced into small strips against the grain

1 cup chung choy, chopped (dried radish, see Tips for Success)

5-6 tablespoons soy sauce

2 teaspoons ginger, grated

1 tablespoon sesame oil

1 tablespoon rice wine vinegar

1 tablespoon potato or corn starch

Black pepper to taste

7-8 green onions, thinly sliced

Hot rice

SERVES: 4-6

Place meat and radish in a bowl. Stir together remaining ingredients, except rice, and pour over meat and radish. Mix well, cover, and refrigerate. Let marinate at least 30 minutes or up to 4 hours.

Pour mixture in a heat-proof dish, cover tightly with aluminum foil, and place in steamer. Steam 8-10 minutes or until meat is done with a slight pink center.

Serve over rice on warm plates.

TIPS FOR SUCCESS

• I was not familiar with chung choy until I learned of this recipe. I found some conflicting information while searching for it. One article tells me it is the salted preserved leaves of the Daikon radish, while another tells me it is the preserved radish itself. Despite searching Asian markets, the internet, and speaking with someone that spoke Cantonese, I was not able to find the preserved leaves. I did, however, find the preserved radish, with and without salt. I prefer the unsalted dried radish for its sweeter flavor. If you can only get salted dried radish, rinse it in several exchanges of water, decrease the amount to ¼-½ cup, and decrease the soy sauce to 3-4 tablespoons.

Chifa is a term you will find in Peru referring to the fusion of Peruvian and Cantonese dishes. There are thousands of Chifa restaurants across Lima and is one of the most popular types of food.

Pasta a la Consuelo

Consuelo's Pasta Sauce

Consuelo took ordinary pasta sauce to a new level by adding her unique twist of Peruvian aji panca. Experiment with various meats: chicken pieces, pork or beef ribs, sausage, etc., or replace the meat with cooked quinoa, and make it a hearty meal.

INGREDIENTS

2 tablespoons olive oil

1 large onion, finely chopped

1 teaspoon salt

½ teaspoon dried oregano

½ teaspoon cumin

1-2 tablespoons aji panca paste, depending on how hot you like it

1 carrot, grated

3 cloves garlic, pressed

2 tomatoes, pureed

8 ounces mushrooms, sliced

1 pound meat

1 (28 ounces) jar of pasta sauce

1 bay leaf

1 pound favorite pasta

Parmesan cheese, freshly grated

SERVES: 4-6

Heat oil in heavy-bottomed sauce pan over medium-high heat, add onion, and sauté 3-4 minutes, stirring frequently until onions just begin to soften.

Add salt, oregano, cumin, aji, and carrot. Stir often and cook another 2-3 minutes. Adjust heat and lower if necessary to keep food from burning.

Add garlic, tomatoes, mushrooms, and meat. Stir and cook 5 minutes. Add pasta sauce and bay leaf. Stir and bring to simmer. Cover and simmer 30 minutes or until meat is fully cooked. Remove bay leaf.

Cook pasta according to package directions and drain.

Serve sauce over pasta on warm plates. Top with grated Parmesan cheese.

Peru has the second largest amount of Shamans in the world, second only to India.

Sweets and Snacks

Especial de Consuelo

Torrejas de Plátano

Mote Tostado

Cancha

Alfajores

Panetón

Santa Catalina Monastery, constructed in 1579, Arequipa, Peru.

Arequipa, Peru, the second most populous region behind Lima, Peru, is lined with a series of volcanic mountains.

La Mansión del Fundador, Arequipa, Peru. This mansion, constructed by the founder of Arequipa, Don Garcí Manuel de Carbajal, is an outstanding example of 16th century architecture, constructed mainly from white volcanic stone. If you have recently visited this site, you may not recognize this photo as the exterior is now painted in an earth-tone orange color.

Especial de Consuelo

Consuelo's Special

This is a fun treat and my husband fondly remembers being sent to the bakery early mornings before school to buy fresh bread. He never complained and hurried out the door. I'm not so sure whether he couldn't wait to get home and enjoy this for breakfast, or to see the cute girl who worked at the bakery?

INGREDIENTS

1 fresh loaf of favorite bread

1 (14 ounce) can of sweetened condensed milk

SERVES: 4-6

Serve bread, tear into pieces, and dip into milk.

Mmmmmm … delicious!

Snow covered Andes as seen from the train
en route to Machu Picchu.

Torrejas de Plátano

Banana Fritters

Don't throw away those overly ripe bananas; they can be transformed into an easy sweet treat for breakfast, snack, or dessert.

INGREDIENTS

¾ cup evaporated milk

2 eggs

3 tablespoons granulated sugar

1 pinch of salt

1½ cups all-purpose flour

2 ice cubes

5 large, very ripe bananas

5 tablespoons vegetable oil, divided

Desired toppings (see Tips for Success)

SERVES: 4-6

In a large mixing bowl, whisk together milk, eggs, sugar, and salt. Add flour and ice cubes and stir well until very smooth and the ice cubes are nearly melted. Remove ice cubes when it reaches a thick pancake-like batter consistency.

Slice bananas very thin and stir into batter, using spoon to break them up a bit.

In a large frying pan, heat 2-3 tablespoons oil over medium-high heat. Pour batter to desired sized fritters and cook until golden. Flip and finish cooking. Repeat with remaining batter, adding more oil as needed. Let cool a few minutes.

Serve with any favorite topping.

TIPS FOR SUCCESS
• The ice cubes have a two-fold purpose in this recipe. First, the ice cubes add some friction when stirring. They break up clumps of flour and help to create a smooth batter. Secondly, they help to control the amount of liquid. You can quickly remove them when the batter reaches the desired consistency.

• Sometimes I add ½ teaspoon of vanilla to the batter and fry them in coconut oil for a little different twist.

• Suggestions for toppings: powdered sugar, honey, butter, maple syrup, cinnamon, crushed nuts, toasted coconut, whipped cream, fresh fruit …

Peru's Independence Day is celebrated on July 28, and is known as 'Fiestas Patrias.'

Mote Tostado

Corn Nuts

Mote is something new we discovered recently in Peru while enjoying a Pisco Sour. Typically cancha is served at bars, but this time it was mote and we really enjoyed it. Mote is made from corn that has been soaked in high alkaline water to remove the hull; in the United States, we know it as hominy. Toasting it makes for a satisfying snack.

INGREDIENTS

1 (15 ounce) bag dried
mote pelado corn

1 teaspoon salt, plus more to taste

2 tablespoons vegetable oil

SERVES: 8-10

Soak mote in enough water to fully cover for 10-12 hours. Drain, rinse, and refresh water. Add 1 teaspoon salt and bring to boil. Cover, reduce heat, and simmer 1½ hours.

Drain well, spread on towel to dry for 15-20 minutes.

Heat oil in a heavy duty pot over medium-high heat. Stir in mote and toast until golden, stirring frequently.

Or, pre-heat oven to 400 degrees F. Drizzle towel dried mote with oil, sprinkle with salt, stir, and spread on a rimmed baking sheet. Bake 20-30 minutes until golden, stirring once or twice.

Place in paper towel lined bowl. Sprinkle with salt and let cool to room temperature.

Serve alongside Pisco Sour or Inca Kola!

Cancha

Toasted Corn

Cancha is Peru's version of popcorn, commonly served with drinks. Be careful, it can be addicting!

INGREDIENTS

1 (15 ounce) bag of Peruvian maiz cancha

2 tablespoons vegetable oil

Salt to taste

SERVES: 8-10

Rinse corn, drain well, and dry on paper towel.

In a medium sized heavy-duty pan, heat oil over medium-high heat. Add corn and stir continually until you begin to hear a cracking sound. Cover pot and continue cooking, shaking pot every 15 seconds. Do this until cracking slows to 3-4 seconds between cracks, about 8-10 minutes, lowering heat to medium if necessary.

Pour into a paper towel lined bowl and add salt to taste. Let cool.

Serve as a snack with a refreshing beverage.

Alfajores

Caramel Filled Almond Cookies

"Beautiful," "A Masterpiece," "Melt in your mouth," "Blissful," "A gift from the gods," are all terms used to describe these sinfully sweet Peruvian cookies. Excellent as an afternoon delight with a cup of tea or coffee. My friends and family constantly request these and they have become my signature recipe!

In our house, we are divided on the best way to enjoy these cookies. My husband likes them when they are first made and the cookies are still crisp. I, on the other hand, like them better the second day after the dulce de leche has had a chance to soften and blend with the cookie. They truly melt in your mouth; it's your choice!

INGREDIENTS

1½ cups unsalted butter, at room temperature

1 cup powdered sugar, plus extra for dusting

2 tablespoons granulated sugar

½ teaspoon almond extract

½ teaspoon vanilla extract

3 cups all-purpose flour

⅓ cup finely ground almonds

½ teaspoon salt

1-1½ cups dulce de leche

Flaked coconut (optional, see Tips for Success)

SERVES

Serves only 1, because no one wants to share!

Using the paddle attachment for your mixer, cream butter with both sugars on high until light and fluffy, about 3-4 minutes, stopping once or twice to scrape down sides. Add both extracts and mix another 30 seconds.

Stir together flour, ground almonds, and salt in a medium bowl. Add to butter and mix on low until combined and mixture begins to form a dough-like ball. Be careful not to over-mix, for it will toughen the dough.

Divide dough into thirds, place each one on plastic wrap, and flatten to a disc shape. Cover tightly with wrap and chill at least 30 minutes, or refrigerate up to 3 days. If your dough is well-chilled, you will need to let it warm a bit before rolling, otherwise it will crack.

Pre-heat oven to 350 degrees F. On a well-floured surface, starting with 1 disc, roll dough to ¼ inch thick. Dip cookie cutter in a small bowl of flour, tapping off excess, and cut dough into desired size rounds. Place on an ungreased cookie sheet. If you have the time, place the sheet of cookies in the refrigerator to chill for 10-15 minutes before placing in the oven. Repeat with remaining dough.

Bake 14-16 minutes or until edges begin to lightly brown. Time varies depending on the size of your cookie, so keep a close eye on them.

Remove from oven and let rest on hot sheet for 1 minute. Remove from sheet with spatula and cool completely on wire rack.

Once cookies are completely cooled, spread a generous amount of dulce de leche on one cookie and top with another cookie to form a sandwich, pressing lightly. Sprinkle heavily with powdered sugar and place on platter.

Serve with café con leche, hot coffee, or tea.

TIPS FOR SUCCESS

• I admit, I usually buy canned dulce de leche because it is much faster than making my own. If dulce de leche is unavailable in your area, it can be made from a can of sweetened condensed milk. The un-opened can must be fully submerged in water. Bring to a boil and maintain boil for 4 hours, adding water as needed to keep it fully submerged at all times! This is extremely important as the can may explode! Carefully remove from water bath. Let cool for several hours before opening and using.

• The best canned dulce de leche is one with a thicker consistency, to hold up on the cookie. Some brands are too runny and can drip out the sides of the cookies.

• Another variation of Alfajores is to gently press on the filled cookie until the caramel slightly protrudes out the side, and then roll the edges in flaked coconut before sprinkling with powdered sugar.

• If you prefer your cookie crisp like my husband does, do not fill the cookies ahead of time. Store them in an airtight container and fill just before eating. Unfilled cookies also freeze well.

• I have experimented with different types of butter and we found a high quality European style butter to be superior to the others. Have fun experimenting to find your favorite butter; no one will complain for having too many test cookies in the house!

• To maintain uniform thickness when rolling dough, I suggest using an adjustable pastry board for perfect results every time.

After a long day of exploring, Armand, Stefan, and Francesca Choy reflect on the nearby sites of Machu Picchu, Peru, from the Sanctuary Lodge.

Panetón

Sweet Christmas Bread

Peru is known for their love of Panetón. To them, it represents Christmas. Like most Peruvians, my husband's family had the tradition of enjoying Panetón on Christmas morning with tea or café con leche. Coincidentally, my mother always made "Christmas Bread," which was our variation of Panetón. Served with tea or coffee, it was also our Christmas breakfast. Little did we know, we were on two different continents sharing the same special delight! This is my version of the sweet and tender holiday bread, made with a sourdough starter. As the tantalizing aroma fills your house, you will never buy the box of Italian Panettone again. Maybe this will become your family's memorable Christmas treat too, "Feliz Navidad!"

INGREDIENTS

2 cups sourdough starter (see Tips for Success)

3 ¼ cups bread flour, divided

½ cup candied fruit, such as orange peel or citron

½ cup golden or dark raisins

¼ cup orange flavored liquor, such as Cointreau or Grand Marnier

¾ cup granulated sugar

2 tablespoons honey

Zest of 3 oranges

Zest of 1 lemon

3 large eggs, room temperature

1 large egg, separated, at room temperature (reserve white for wash)

1 teaspoon vanilla or seeds from 1 vanilla bean pod

9 tablespoons unsalted butter,

divided and at room temperature

1 teaspoon salt

½ cup roughly chopped almonds

1 egg wash (optional)

2 tablespoons pearl sugar (optional)

SERVES: 8-10

"Windowpane effect" for Panetón

Great Panetón starts with a very wet dough.

THE NIGHT BEFORE:

Start by preparing your sourdough sponge: mix 2 cups of sourdough starter with 1 ¼ cup flour. Using a mixer with an attached dough hook, knead on low for 5 minutes. Cover with warm damp towel and let rest 8 hours in a draft free location (I put mine in a cool oven overnight to keep the air conditioning from blowing on it).

Mix candied fruit and raisins with liqueur to soak for at least 8 hours. Cover and set aside for later. Place butter on counter to warm to room temperature for morning.

IN THE MORNING:

Place eggs in a bowl of hot water for 5-10 minutes to bring them to room temperature.

Once the sponge has proofed overnight, add 1 ½ cups flour, sugar, honey, zest, 3 eggs, 1 yolk, and vanilla. Using mixer, knead on low for 10 minutes. Add more flour, a tablespoon at a time, if needed; you may end up adding the entire last ½ cup depending on your climate. It will begin to slightly pull away from sides, but it should not form a ball; this is meant to be a wet dough.

Using 8 tablespoons of butter, add 1 tablespoon at a time, and mix 15-20 seconds in-between additions to make sure it is well-incorporated. Set aside the last tablespoon of butter for later.

Add salt and knead another 5 minutes on low. The dough should be shiny and smooth, but should not produce a translucent windowpane effect just yet. Cover bowl with a warm damp towel and place in a draft-free location for 1 hour. The dough should rise, but not quite double.

Add soaked fruit, nuts, and all liquid. Do not drain; the liqueur adds important flavor! Knead an additional 8-10 minutes. At this point the dough should be beautiful, smooth, and shiny. It now should create a perfect windowpane effect when stretched.

Pour dough into an ungreased 9-10 inch tube pan. Spread dough evenly and cover with a warm damp towel. Place in a warm, draft-free location to rise until doubled in volume, about 4 hours, depending on the speed of your sourdough (this time I place it in my oven with the light on to create a little more warmth).

Pre-heat oven to 375 degrees F. Remember to remove the dough from oven while pre-heating!

Once the dough has risen, carefully place the last tablespoon of butter on top in small thin pats, or brush gently with an egg white wash if you prefer a sheen. Sprinkle with pearl sugar (if using), and place on the bottom rack of the pre-heated oven. Set timer for 10 minutes, reduce heat to 350, and bake another 35-45 minutes until internal temperature reaches 190 degrees F.

This next step is probably the most important step, so please do not skip! Immediately after removing from oven, turn pan upside down to cool completely for at least 2-3 hours (see Tips for Success).

Once cool, using a spatula or knife, loosen sides and carefully remove from tube pan. Place on a beautiful cake plate.

Serve with café con leche, hot coffee or tea, or wrap tightly in plastic wrap for later use.

TIPS FOR SUCCESS

• Sourdough … nature's ancient yeasts! If you are not familiar with sourdough, do some research before attempting this recipe. You will need to purchase sourdough starter, or find a friend who already has active starter. I'm sure they will be more than happy to share.

• The reason for cooling the bread upside down is to keep its tall structure and airiness. If cooled right side up, it would collapse and become dense.

• Some tube pans come equipped with metal feet to allow it to rest upside down. If yours does not have this feature, it can be placed upside down on a cooling rack, if the top of the bread hasn't risen above the edge, or inverted over a long neck bottle.

• I prefer a tube pan for this bread because it allows the center to bake nicely without the outside becoming dry.

• If you are lucky enough to have any leftovers, I hear it makes a wonderful French toast or bread pudding. I've yet to have that opportunity!

• My mother also prepared the same bread in the spring, placed jelly beans on top after baking and titled it "Easter bread." She would create a holiday colored glaze with powdered sugar and milk to drizzle over the bread after it cooled. Red or green for Christmas, and purple or pink for Easter.

• I like to experiment with various flavor combinations. Recently I made a Piña colada version: I soaked candied pineapple and golden raisins in coconut flavored rum rather than the orange based liqueur. I omitted the orange and lemon zest, and replaced the almonds with macadamia nuts. Just before baking, I topped it with pats of butter, and sprinkled it with sweetened coconut for a very nice tropical taste.

I ♥ PERUVIAN FOOD

Lomo Saltado

Menu Suggestions

NOW THAT YOU HAVE THESE RECIPES, what do you do with them? You want to get started, but you're not quite sure how. Begin by trying some of these sample menus, or put together your own combinations based on your likes, dislikes, and cooking ability. You will see that I chose Lomo Saltado often for the main dish. First of all, Lomo Saltado has Peruvian written all over it and is a standard on most Peruvian menus. Secondly, it is very easy to make! The forward slash means for you to decide how many foods to prepare.

Always keep in mind the reason for opening your home and your heart: to gather around the table to enjoy the company of your family and friends. It doesn't have to be perfect; it just has to be full of warmth and hospitality. Remember, the secret is to put your love into every dish, and celebrate mealtime everyday!

Come join us on a culinary adventure,
Katie and Consuelo

Salud,

Katie Choy

There are 3 official languages in Peru: Spanish, Quechua, and Aymara, but east of the Andes in Amazon jungle regions, it is thought that natives speak a further 13 different languages.

▦ Worst case scenario – you need something easy, yet traditional, but have no access to Peruvian ingredients or have no time to order:

DRINKS: Té Helado

STARTERS: Papa a la Huancaina using jalapeños

MAIN DISH: Lomo Saltado with frozen French fries

DESSERT: Especial de Consuelo with Café con Leche

▦ You have full access to ingredients but are looking for a very easy-to-prepare dinner:

DRINKS: Inca Kola/Pisco Sours

STARTERS: Anticuchos

MAIN DISH: Aji de Gallina, slow-cooker version

DESSERT: Especial de Consuelo with Café con Leche

Typical Peruvian "Peña".

■ You have full access to ingredients and are willing to try something that is a bit more time consuming but not overwhelming:

DRINKS: Chicha Morada/Pisco Sour

STARTERS: Papa a la Huancaina/Ocopa con Papas

MAIN DISH: Lomo Saltado

DESSERT: Alfajores with Café con Leche

■ You are ready for anything, including a full-blown fiesta with very traditional choices:

DRINKS: Inca Kola cocktails/Pisco Sour/Chicha Morada/Té Helado

SNACKS: Cancha/Mote

1ST STARTERS: Ceviche/Causa Rellena, both can be served as individual bite-sized portions

2ND STARTERS: Papa Rellena/Anticuchos/Empanadas

MAIN DISH: Lomo Saltado/Aji de Gallina/Escabeche de Pollo

SIDES: White Rice/Arroz Amarillo

DESSERT: Alfajores/Especial de Consuelo with Café con Leche

Holiday Menu:

DRINKS: Chicha Morada with
sparkling water/Pisco Sour

STARTERS: Ceviche/Caldo de Pollo con Wontons

MAIN MEAL: Asado de Cerdo with
Puré de Papa/Aji de Gallina

DESSERT: Panetón with Café con Leche

Hot Lunch Menu:

DRINKS: Chicha Morada/Té Helado/
Café con Leche

STARTERS: Empanadas/Anticuchos

MAIN DISH: Escabeche de Pollo

DESSERT: Alfajores with Café con Leche

Cold Lunch Menu:

DRINKS: Chicha Morada/Té Helado

STARTERS: Ceviche

MAIN DISH: Causa Rellena

DESSERT: Alfajores with Café con Leche

Interactive party where your guests put on an apron, roll up their sleeves, and participate in the cooking:

DRINKS: Pisco Sours

SNACKS: Mote/Cancha

STARTERS: Empanadas/Papa Rellena

MAIN MEAL: Lomo Saltado

DESSERT: Alfajores with Café con Leche

TIPS FOR SUCCESS

• The best way to entertain is to have your day well-planned by being proactive and by doing as much of the prep as you can ahead of time. Make menu choices within your ability, and don't try to go beyond your level of comfort. Otherwise, everyone will sense your stress. Your guests should feel as if it was effortless, and you should be enjoying their company as well as enjoying the meal yourself.

• Stir-fry foods are best eaten fresh rather than re-heated. If you have your prep done early, the cook-time itself is brief and is easily done while your guests are present. In fact, most enjoy watching the process and their mouths will be watering, anticipating the flavors.

• When hosting a full-blown dinner party, I have one suggestion: hire help!

• Interactive parties are so much fun! It is a way to serve some of the more labor-intensive foods without having the stress of doing it all yourself. It still requires some preparation ahead of time, like having the mote/cancha made so everyone can snack while working, and having the meat filling and dough ready. Don't be afraid to assign specific jobs: one can be squeezing limes and blending the Pisco sours, while others are filling empanadas and papa rellena. If you choose to make papa rellena, the frying can be very dangerous, and I would not recommend allowing your guests near the hot oil. Pre-bake Alfajores, but allow your guests to fill and top their own. I guarantee it will be an evening full of messy hands and lots of laughter!

The oldest occupation of man in the Americas is traced back to the sacred City of Caral-Supe a few hours north of the capital Lima. The 626 hectare (1546 acre) site dates back 5000 years.

The Royal Tomb of Machu Picchu, Peru, a site of numerous mummy excavations.

Index

Golden statue of ancient Inca warrior

Peru is the 6th largest producer of gold.